MASSES WITH YOUNG PEOPLE

Masses with Young People

Sr. Jude Groden RSM
Rev. Christopher O'Donnell O.CARM

McCrimmons
Great Wakering, Essex, England

Dedicated to Religious Educators, School Chaplains and Catechists in their challenging roles.

Nihil Obstat: Mgr. George Stokes
                  Censor Deputatus

Imprimatur: + Thomas McMahon
                  Bishop of Brenwood

First published in United Kingdom in 2006 by
McCrimmon Publishing Co. Ltd.,
10-12 High Street, Great Wakering, Essex SS3 0EQ
info@mccrimmons.com
www.mccrimmons.com

© 2006 Sr Jude Groden RSM and Rev Christopher O.Donnell O.CARM

ISBN 0 85597 680 2

Acknowledgements

Scriptural extracts and responsorial psalms are taken from the *Good News Bible* published by The Bible Societies/Harper Collins Publishers Ltd., UK. © American Bible Society 1966, 1971, 1976, 1992.
Addresses for copyright holders of the words for hymns used in this publication can be found on page 136.

Every effort has been made to trace the owners of copyright material and we hope that no copyright has been infringed. Pardon is sought and apology made if the contrary be the case, and a correction will be made in any reprint of this book.

Cover photograph by Alan Hencher
Cover illustration by The Benedictine Sisters of Turvey Abbey
Cover, page design and layout by Nick Snode
Typeset in 11 and 11.5pt Verdana
Printed and bound by Thanet Press Ltd., Margate, Kent

CONTENTS

FOREWORD 7

INTRODUCTION 8

1 SEASONS

ADVENT 12
    Liturgy
    Teacher's Notes
    Celebrant's Notes

EPIPHANY 16
    Liturgy
    Teacher's Notes
    Celebrant's Notes

CANDLEMAS
PRESENTATION OF THE LORD 20
    Liturgy
    Teacher's Notes
    Celebrant's Notes

LENT 24
    Liturgy
    Teacher's Notes
    Celebrant's Notes

EASTER 28
    Liturgy
    Teacher's Notes
    Celebrant's Notes

ASCENSION 32
    Liturgy
    Teacher's Notes
    Celebrant's Notes

CORPUS CHRISTI 36
    Liturgy
    Teacher's Notes
    Celebrant's Notes

PENTECOST 40
    Liturgy
    Teacher's Notes
    Celebrant's Notes

2 FEASTS

OUR LADY 44
    Liturgy
    Teacher's Notes
    Celebrant's Notes

ALL SAINTS 48
    Liturgy
    Teacher's Notes
    Celebrant's Notes

REMEMBRANCE 52
    Liturgy
    Teacher's Notes
    Celebrant's Notes

OUR LADY OF LOURDES 56
    Liturgy
    Teacher's Notes
    Celebrant's Notes

ST DAVID 60
    Liturgy
    Teacher's Notes
    Celebrant's Notes

ST PATRICK   64
Liturgy
Teacher's Notes
Celebrant's Notes

ST JOSEPH   68
Liturgy
Teacher's Notes
Celebrant's Notes

ST GEORGE   70
Liturgy
Teacher's Notes
Celebrant's Notes

SS PETER & PAUL   76
Liturgy
Teacher's Notes
Celebrant's Notes

ST ANDREW   80
Liturgy
Teacher's Notes
Celebrant's Notes

3 OCCASIONS

OPENING OF THE SCHOOL YEAR   84
Liturgy
Teacher's Notes
Celebrant's Notes

HARVEST   88
Liturgy
Teacher's Notes
Celebrant's Notes

CHRISTIAN UNITY   92
Liturgy
Teacher's Notes
Celebrant's Notes

PEACE & RECONCILIATION   96
Liturgy
Teacher's Notes
Celebrant's Notes

FIRST COMMUNION   100
Liturgy
Teacher's Notes
Celebrant's Notes

SCHOOL LEAVERS   104
Liturgy
Teacher's Notes
Celebrant's Notes

ANNIVERSARY OF SCHOOL   108
Liturgy
Teacher's Notes
Celebrant's Notes

INSPECTION TIME   112
Liturgy
Teacher's Notes
Celebrant's Notes

RETIREMENT   116
Liturgy
Teacher's Notes
Celebrant's Notes

LOCAL & NATIONAL TRAGEDY   122
Liturgy
Teacher's Notes
Celebrant's Notes

DEATH OF A PUPIL   124
Liturgy
Teacher's Notes
Celebrant's Notes

MASS FOR A SUICIDE VICTIM   128
Liturgy
Teacher's Notes
Celebrant's Notes

CLOSING OF SCHOOL YEAR   132
Liturgy
Teacher's Notes
Celebrant's Notes

FOREWORD

Sr. Jude Groden, a Mercy sister and Religious Advisor in the Brentwood diocese, and Fr. Christopher O'Donnell, an Irish Carmelite theologian from the Milltown Institute, Dublin, have come together once more to help those involved in religious education and with young people to explore the mysteries of spirituality and prayer.

In this book they seek to help teachers and celebrants to prepare for Masses with young people. They recognise that there can be pressures of time or circumstances when a ready-made liturgy might be very welcome. But they are more concerned to help those dealing with young people to draw out the riches of the Mass for special occasions and for ordinary celebrations.

I welcome in particular their creative suggestions of symbols and thoughts. Those attending Mass can carry these away with them after the celebration. The wide-ranging Bidding Prayers also show how the Mass is integrated into the whole of life and society.

Six months before he died Pope John Paul II proclaimed a year of the Eucharist. In his Apostolic Letter, *Mane nobiscum Domine* (Stay with us Lord), he asked the bishops to encourage initiatives on a deeply spiritual level that will anchor pastoral programmes "in the very Mystery which nourishes the spiritual life of the faithful and the initiatives of each local Church... and to emphasise the Eucharistic dimension which is part of the whole Christian life" (n.5).

I welcome and commend this book and feel it will be a useful tool especially for priests and teachers.

† Thomas McMahon.

BISHOP OF BRENTWOOD

INTRODUCTION

THE MASS is a central mystery of our faith. Since it is a mystery, we cannot at any time fully understand it. There are so many ways of approaching it. We can turn the Mass around in our minds, each time seeing something new and special, some greater wonder. *The Catechism of the Catholic Church* (nn.1328-1332) offers us ten names for the sacrament, each indicating a different aspect.

○ The *EUCHARIST*, from a Greek word meaning thanksgiving, because we proclaim and give thanks for God's creation, redemption and sanctification.

○ The *LORD'S SUPPER,* since it is connected with Jesus' last meal with his disciples the day before he suffered and died for us.

○ The *BREAKING OF BREAD,* since Jesus did this at the Last Supper: he took bread, blessed, broke and gave it to his disciples. Later Christians were recognised as those "who broke bread."

○ The *EUCHARISTIC ASSEMBLY,* because it is the celebration of the believing community to hear God's word and to celebrate the Mystery.

○ The *MEMORIAL* of the Lord's Passion and Resurrection.

○ The *HOLY SACRIFICE,* as it makes present the one sacrifice of Christ on the Cross for our redemption.

○ The *HOLY AND DIVINE LITURGY,* since it is the centre and the greatest act of the Church's worship.

○ We call the Eucharist, *THE BLESSED SACRAMENT* as it is the greatest of all the sacraments.

○ It is *HOLY COMMUNION,* since it unites us to Christ in his Body and Blood, making us all one body.

○ It is *HOLY MASS,* from the fact that there is a sending (*missio*) from the liturgy to the world in service.

All this mystery cannot be taken in at once. But we can approach this centre of our faith in different ways.

Masses with Young People

▨ Teachers and priests will recognise both the opportunity and the difficulties of celebrating Mass with young people. The opportunities are there to share the word of God with them, to pray with them, to offer the Church's sacrifice with them. The Mass is worship, but it can also be catechesis and evangelisation.

But there are also difficulties and challenges. It is hard to be endlessly creative, and young people like what is fresh and new. Again there is not always time to prepare as frequently: a school event, a feast, may creep up on us and there will be a pressure to get ready.

The aim of this book is to help young people to integrate their lives with their worship. It consists of thirty-one Masses. They are arranged for seasons, feasts and special school occasions. Each Mass is complete and requires only a copy of the appropriate Eucharistic Prayer. Hymns are supplied, but can be replaced by others.

Features of the Masses

▨ There are three parts to each of these Masses. Firstly there is a complete text for the celebration.

There is a section of NOTES FOR TEACHERS, give some background for the celebration, a central focus for Mass on this particular occasion, indications about the readings, a word about a possible preface and Eucharistic prayer, and some indication how those who have shared in the Mass can carry its values and gifts with them into daily life.

Thirdly, there are NOTES FOR THE CELEBRANT. These may help teachers and the priest to approach a Mass in a broadly similar way. Again there are background notes with introduction, pointers to the readings, homily hints, a Communion reflection and a sending-away thought.

Parts of the Mass

▨ In preparing the notes for teachers and celebrants the authors sought to integrate catechetical material, so that young people may come to a deeper understanding of the Mass.

Each Mass has BACKGROUND NOTES. Information about feasts and celebrations, or the lives of saints may not always be easily to hand, so these are supplied. Again, situations like school inspections, a liturgical season, a tragedy or a saint may be viewed in many ways. The background notes are meant to suggest some ideas; hopefully they will lead teachers and priests to other, deeper, more contextualised thoughts that will speak to those who take part in the celebration. The central focus in the notes for teachers is meant also to provoke creativity amongst the teacher and the young people as they prepare the Mass together.

There is a spiritual power in SCRIPTURE READINGS. They do, however, need an introduction to place them in the totality God's message. There could be a danger that if there is too much suggested, those attending will only have a blurred impression of what is in the readings. Hence these have been kept short.

The INTERCESSIONS are a catechesis in prayer. They show how everything can be brought to God in prayer, most suitably at Mass.

The RESPONSES offered in place of the customary, *"Lord graciously hear us"* or *"Lord hear our prayer,"* are meant to suggest little prayer formulae that can be used later apart from Mass. In the years before Vatican II Catholics were accustomed to use aspirations like "Sacred Heart of Jesus, I place my trust in you" or "O Mary conceived without sin, pray for us who have recourse to thee." Now that this practice of aspirations is not longer widespread, there are distinct possibilities of teaching young people to use phrases of scripture, or other prayer formulae in the ups and downs of daily life.

It is important to emphasise the PREFACE and the EUCHARISTIC PRAYER. These are the great prayers of thanksgiving from which "Eucharist" gets its name. The preface is addressed to God and gives the reasons why *today* we should enter into adoration and thanksgiving.

The COMMUNION REFLECTIONS must not cut across the way that people are drawn to Jesus in mind and heart. There would be a time of silence as well as music. But before the silence ends there can be a real value in indicating some way of listening and speaking to Jesus that arises out of the Mass that has been celebrated. Teachers and priests who know that young people

gathered for the Mass will be in a position to offer short reflections of a sentence or so.

These Mass texts with their notes will hopefully be developed in a creative way by teachers whose own insights and experience will modify, adapt or ignore some of what is offered here. The authors are very grateful to teachers who have commented on their previous volumes of *School Assemblies* and on praying with scripture. Their observations have encouraged the production of these Masses. The authors also thank Ms. Mary Cronin and Mgr. George Stokes for valuable and generous help in the production of the book. They are especially grateful to the Rt. Rev. Thomas McMahon, Bishop of Brentwood who graciously contributed a foreword to this book.

In offering this book to teachers and priests the authors echo a phrase of the New Testament, which can surely be applied to the Eucharist: "Great indeed is the mystery of our religion" (1 Tim 3:16).

1 | SEASONS

ADVENT

1 LITURGY

Opening hymn

Come, Lord Jesus, Light of nations
Glory Jesus Christ (x2)
Glory, hallelujah, glory Jesus Christ! (x2)
Come, Lord Jesus, born of Mary
Glory...
Come, and show the Father's glory
Glory...

[Celebration Hymnal for Everyone no.8]

© 1974 Shalom Community, 1504 Polk, Wichitaw Falls, Texas 76309, USA

INTRODUCTORY RITES

Greeting

Penitential Rite

Lord Jesus, you come to save us.

R/. Lord have mercy.

Lord Jesus, you are the Son of God.

R/. Christ have mercy

Lord Jesus, you are the rainbow of God's love
and mercy.

R/. Lord have mercy.

Opening prayer

God our Father, help us to prepare well for the coming of your Son at Christmas and at the end of time. We ask this through Jesus Christ our Lord who lives and reigns with you and the Holy Spirit one God for ever and ever.

R/. Amen.

■ LITURGY OF THE WORD

First Reading   *Isaiah 9:2-3,6-7*

The people that walked in darkness have seen a great light. They lived in a land of shadows, but now light is shining on them. You have given them great joy, Lord; you have made them happy. They rejoice in what you have done, as people rejoice when they harvest their corn or when they divide captured wealth. A child is born to us! A Son is given to us! And he will be our ruler. He will be called, "Wonderful Counsellor," "Mighty God," "Eternal Father," "Prince of Peace." His royal power will continue to grow; His Kingdom will always be at peace. He will rule as King David's successor, basing his power on right and justice, from now until the end of time.

This is the Word of the Lord.

R/. Thanks be to God

Responsorial Psalm   *Psalm 80*

*R/. Show us your mercy
    and we will be saved.*

Listen to us, O Shepherd of Israel;
Hear us, leader of your flock
Seated on your throne above the winged
    creatures
Show us your strength; come and save us.

*R/. Show us your mercy
    and we will be saved.*

Turn to us, Almighty God!
Look down from heaven at us;
Come and save your people!
Come and save this grapevine that you
    planted.

*R/. Show us your mercy
    and we will be saved.*

Preserve and protect the people you have
    chosen,
The nation that you made strong.
We will never turn away from you again;
Keep us alive and we will praise you.

*R/. Show us your mercy
    and we will be saved.*

Gospel Acclamation   *Sung*

Alleluia, Alleluia,
Come Lord Jesus
Alleluia, Alleluia.

Gospel   *Matthew 3:1-6*

At that time John the Baptist came to the desert of Judea and started preaching: "Turn away from your sins," he said, "because the Kingdom of heaven is near. People came to him from the whole province of Judea, and from all the country near the River Jordan. They confessed their sins, and he baptised them in the Jordan.

This is the Gospel of the Lord.

R/. Praise to you, Lord Jesus Christ.

Prayer of the Faithful

[Celebrant] We pray for the coming of the Lord.

R/. Come and save us.

Jesus, our Saviour, our Church and world yearn for your coming.

R/. Come and save us.

For all of us who long for your coming this Christmas.

R/. Come and save us.

For all those who are seeking meaning in their lives.

R/. Come and save us.

For all with family pain and difficulties at this time.

R/. Come and save us.

For this school community and parish.

R/. Come and save us.

[Celebrant] Open our eyes O God to see our need for you, and to welcome you into our lives.

R/. Amen.

■ LITURGY OF THE EUCHARIST

Preparation of the Altar and procession with the Gifts   *Music*

Prayer over the Gifts

Lord, may the power of the Spirit,
make holy the gifts we place upon this altar
and prepare us to celebrate your coming
at Christmas.
We ask this through Christ our Lord.

R/. Amen.

Eucharistic Prayer   *Children II*

13

Prayer after Communion

Lord strengthen us by the Sacrament we have received.
Help us to go out to meet our Saviour with open hearts.
We ask this in the name of Jesus the Lord.

R/. Amen.

Blessing

Dismissal

Recessional hymn

"How lovely on the mountains"

[Celebration Hymnal for Everyone no.268]

2 TEACHER'S NOTES

Background

THERE are many things we take for granted: air, clean water, health. Sometimes we only learn to appreciate them when we are without. The Jews longed for the coming of the Messiah. We reflect with them, reading the Old Testament promises with them. In this way we try to appreciate what a gift we have in God-who-is-with-us, Emmanuel. The two Advent people are John the Baptist who prepared the way for the Lord, and Mary who who looked forward to the birth of her Son.

Central focus

God comes to us in the Eucharist in Christ Jesus. He speaks his word to us, teaches and instructs us.

Readings

The two readings are about different stages of preparation for the Lord. The first is an Old Testament text that expresses the people's longing for the Messiah. He is described in beautiful language: "Wonderful Counsellor, Mighty God, Eternal Father, Prince of Peace." The Gospel tells of the immediate preparation for the mission of Jesus. John prepares the way for him by calling on people to repent and to be baptised.

Offertory

Procession with symbols and gifts
- ❍ Advent wreath
- ❍ Symbols for Jesse tree.
- ❍ Purple drape
- ❍ Figures for crib (excluding child).
- ❍ Bread and wine which the Holy Spirit will overshadow to give us the Body and Blood of the Lord.

Eucharistic prayer

The Church gives thanks in the Eucharistic prayer that God loves us and sent Jesus to us. Through the Holy Spirit he continually comes at Mass.

Holy Holy	*Sung*
Memorial acclamation	*Sung*
Great Amen	*Sung*
Communion	*Music*

Follow up

Every time we see the word "Christmas" we should be conscious of the first six letters, C H R I S T; he must be the centre of the celebration.

▣ CELEBRANT'S NOTES

Background

INTRODUCTION TO THE MASS

WE ARE all used to different years. The football year starts about August; the civil year in January; the cricket year in April; the Church's year in late November or early December. Advent has been celebrated in the West since the sixth century. It begins on the Sunday nearest the feast of St Andrew.

The four weeks before Christmas are a time of preparation when we think of the three comings of Christ. We know that Jesus has already come. We look forward to his coming at the end of time. Meanwhile we celebrate his presence amongst us in grace and in the Eucharist. But if we are to appreciate his coming, it is helpful to reflect for a month with the Jewish people who longed for the Messiah. The two great Advent figures are John the Baptist who prepared the way for the Lord, and Mary.

Readings

The great prophecy of Isaiah looks to the coming of the Messiah "Wonderful Counsellor, Mighty God, Eternal Father, Prince of Peace." We should enter somehow into the longing the people had for a saviour.
The Gospel text shows the preaching of John the Baptist, who calls on people to repent.

Homily pointers

Emmanuel – God-with-us
○ Finding Christ at Christmas.
○ Preparation for Christmas is turning to God in repentance and love.
○ The Christmas gift is Jesus – can we share him?
○ John the Baptist points to Jesus' coming.
○ Mary brings Jesus into the world.
○ "Your eternal Word has brought to the eyes of faith a new and radiant vision of your glory. In him we see our God made visible, and so are caught up in love of the God we cannot see."

[Christmas Preface 1]

Communion reflection

Thank you Jesus for coming to me.
Look on those who are lost
and do not know you.
Help me to love you as you deserve.
Come Lord Jesus.

Dismissal

A parting thought: Keep looking at the first part of Christmas: C H R I S T.

[Thanks to those who prepared the liturgy and participated in it.]

EPIPHANY

1 LITURGY

Opening hymn

We three Kings of Orient are;
bearing gifts we traverse afar;
field and fountain, moor and mountain,
following yonder star.

O star of wonder, star of night,
star of royal beauty bright
Westward leading, still proceeding,
guide us to thy perfect light.

[Celebration Hymnal for Everyone no.788]

■ INTRODUCTORY RITES

Greeting

Penitential

Lord Jesus, star of wonder
who leads us to you.
R/. Lord have mercy.

Lord Jesus, star of night
who shows us love.
R/. Christ have mercy.

Lord Jesus, star of royal beauty
who guides our ways.
R/. Lord have mercy.

Gloria

Opening prayer

Wondrous God you revealed Jesus to the
world by the guidance of a star.
Help us to become more like him.
We ask this through our Lord Jesus Christ,
your Son, who lives and reigns with you and
the Holy Spirit, one God, for ever and ever.
R/. Amen.

■ LITURGY OF THE WORD

First Reading
Isaiah 60:1-6

Arise, Jerusalem, and shine like the sun; the glory of the Lord is shining on you! Other nations will be covered by darkness, but on you the light of the Lord will shine; the brightness of his presence will be with you. Nations will be drawn to your light, and kings to the dawning of your new day. Look around you and see what is happening: Your people are gathering to come home! Your sons will come from far away; your daughters will be carried like children. You will see this and be filled with joy; you will tremble with excitement. The wealth of the nations will be brought to you; from across the sea their riches will come. Great caravans of camels will come from Midian and Ephah. They will come from Sheba, bringing gold and incense. People will tell the good news of what the Lord has done!

This is the Word of the Lord.
R/. Thanks be to God.

Responsorial Psalm
Psalm 71

R/. All nations will fall prostrate before you, O Lord.

O God, give your judgement to the King,
to a king's son your justice,
that he may judge people in justice
And your poor in right judgement.
R/. All nations will fall prostrate before you, O Lord.

In his days justice shall flourish
and peace till the moon fails.
He shall rule from sea to sea
from the great river to earth's bounds.
R/. All nations will fall prostrate before you, O Lord.

The Kings of Tarshish and the sea coasts
shall pay him tribute.
The Kings of Sheba and Seba
shall bring him gifts.

Before him all Kings shall fall prostrate
all nations shall serve him.

   *R/. All nations will fall prostrate before you,
   O Lord.*

Second Reading   *Ephesians 3:2-3,5-6*

Surely you have heard that God in his grace has given me this work to do for your good. God revealed his secret plan and made it known to me. In past times mankind was not told this secret but God has revealed it now by the Spirit to his holy apostles and prophets. The secret is that by means of the Gospel the gentiles have a part with the Jews in God's blessing; they are members of the same body and share in the promise that God made through Jesus Christ.

This is the Word of the Lord.

   R/. Thanks be to God.

Gospel Acclamation   *Sung*

   Alleluia, Alleluia!
   We saw his star as it rose and we have come
      to do the Lord homage.
   Alleluia.

Gospel   *Matthew 2: 1-12*

Jesus was born in the town of Bethlehem in Judea, during the time when Herod was king. Soon afterwards, some men who studied the stars came from the east to Jerusalem and asked, "Where is the baby born to be the king of the Jews? We saw his star when it came up in the east, and we have come to worship him." When Herod heard about this, he was very upset, and so was everyone else in Jerusalem. He called together all the chief priests and the teachers of the Law and asked them, "Where will the Messiah be born?" "In the town of Bethlehem in Judea," they answered. "For this is what the prophet wrote: 'Bethlehem in the land of Judah, you are by no means the least of the leading cities of Judah; for from you will come a leader who will guide my people Israel.'"
So Herod called the visitors from the east to a secret meeting and found out from them the exact time the star had appeared. Then he sent them to Bethlehem with these instructions: "Go and make a careful search for the child, and

when you find him, let me know, so that I too may go and worship him." And so they left, and on their way they saw the same star they had seen in the east. When they saw it, how happy they were, what joy was theirs! It went ahead of them until it stopped over the place where the child was. They went into the house, and when they saw the child with his mother Mary, they knelt down and worshipped him. They brought out their gifts of gold, frankincense, and myrrh, and presented them to him. Then they returned to their country by another road, since God had warned them in a dream not to go back to Herod.

This is the Gospel of the Lord.

   R/. Praise to you, Lord Jesus Christ.

Creed

Prayer of the Faithful

[Celebrant] God of light and wonder draw near to us as we pray.

   *R/. We saw his star as it rose
   and we have come to worship him.*

That we may seek the gifts of wonder and adoration.

   *R/. We saw his star as it rose
   and we have come to worship him.*

That we may love all people.

   *R/. We saw his star as it rose
   and we have come to worship him.*

That we may be generous and welcoming to strangers.

   *R/. We saw his star as it rose
   and we have come to worship him.*

That we may, with the Wise Men, take time in prayer to bow down and adore you.

   *R/. We saw his star as it rose
   and we have come to worship him.*

[Celebrant] God of all nations hear these prayers which we make with confidence that you long to show yourself to us.
We ask this through Christ our Lord.

   R/. Amen.

▤ LITURGY OF THE EUCHARIST

Preparation of the Altar and procession with the Gifts *Music*

Prayer over the Gifts

Lord, accept the offerings of your Church, not gold, frankincense and myrrh, but the sacrifice and food they symbolise:
Jesus Christ, who is Lord forever and ever.
R/. Amen.

Eucharistic Prayer

Jesus, Way to the Father

Prayer after Communion

Father, guide us with your light, help us to recognise Christ in this Eucharist and welcome him with love, for he is Lord forever and ever.
R/. Amen.

Blessing

Dismissal

Recessional hymn

"Go, tell it on the mountain"

[Celebration Hymnal for Everyone no.202]

2 TEACHER'S NOTES

Background

THE WORD "Epiphany" means appearance. People queue for hours to get a glimpse of a pop-star, a sporting personality, a member of the Royal Family. The famous person passes by – it is all over in less than a minute.

The notable personage will not remember his or her fans, but the fan may keep the encounter in mind for years. In the Church's liturgy three epiphanies are noted: the appearance to the wise men at Bethlehem; Jesus' manifestation to his disciples at Cana (see John 2:1-10); his manifestation to the Jewish people at his baptism (see Matt 3:13-17; Mark 1:9-11; Luke 21-22). The wise men are traditionally given the names of Casper, Balthasar and Melchior. The three gifts have a meaning: gold to show that Jesus is King, incense that he is Son of God, myrrh that he will die.

Central focus

The wise men were risk-takers. They saw a star and were faithful to it, following it until it brought them to Jesus. We can imagine their doubts, their wonderings. They found their security in the star. We find security in the Eucharist that instructs and strengthens us.

Offertory

Procession with symbols and gifts:
- ○ Star.
- ○ Crib figures of the three wise men.
- ○ Three wrapped gifts.
- ○ Bread and wine: our gift to God who will change them utterly to be our food.

Eucharistic Prayer

The Eucharistic prayer leads us to Jesus who is found with Mary. Our gifts of bread and wine become the greatest Gift, Jesus Christ.

Holy Holy	*Sung*
Memorial Acclamation	*Sung*
Great Amen	*Sung*
Communion	*Sung*

Follow up

What is our star?
What are our deepest desires?
Can we ask Jesus help us to attain them?

3 CELEBRANT'S NOTES

Background

INTRODUCTION TO MASS

IN THE Eastern Churches they first celebrated the feast of the Lord's baptism, which was an Epiphany, meaning appearance. Later they added the feast of Christmas; then in both East and West we have three manifestations, as the hymn has it:

> Manifested by the star
> To the sages from afar...
> Manifest at Jordan's stream
> Prophet Priest and King supreme,
> And at Cana wedding guest
> In thy Godhead manifest.

In the celebration we can look at how Jesus was manifested, at how others found him.

Readings

The first reading from Isaiah looks to the glory of the Messiah that is to come. The Ephesians reading brings us into mystery: God's plan, long hidden and now revealed. The Gospel gives the story of the wise men.

Homily pointers

Manifestation:

- ❍ How God shows himself to people – Bethlehem, Cana, Baptism.
- ❍ How people must search and be constant like the wise men.
- ❍ The gifts to bring to Jesus, Mary and Joseph: our hearts alive and loving.
- ❍ How we remember seeing somebody famous.
- ❍ Our star? Will our desires bring us to God?
- ❍ "Finding God in all things" (St Ignatius Loyola).

Communion reflection

Jesus, thank you for your love.
Jesus, keep me on track.
Jesus, keep me going.
Jesus, show me yourself and your will.

Dismissal

A parting thought: How will you find Jesus today?

[Thanks to those who prepared the liturgy and participated in it.]

CANDLEMAS / PRESENTATION OF THE LORD

1 LITURGY

Opening hymn

The light of Christ
Has come into the world *(x2)*
The light of God has come to us,
So that we might have salvation;
From the darkness of our sins we walk
Into glory with Christ Jesus.

[Celebration Hymnal for Everyone no.703]

© 1974 The Word of God Music / Administered by Copycare. Used by permission.

◼ INTRODUCTORY RITES

Greeting

Penitential Rite

Lord Jesus, you are the light of the world.
  R/. Lord have mercy.

Lord Jesus, you lead us from darkness to light.
  R/. Christ have mercy

Lord Jesus, you open our hearts to your light and love.
  R/. Lord have mercy

Gloria

Opening prayer

Creator of light, Christ your Son became one of us and was presented in the temple. May he free us from all selfishness and bring us into the light of your presence. We ask this through Jesus Christ our Lord who lives and reigns with you and the Holy Spirit, one God, for ever and ever.
  R/. Amen.

◼ LITURGY OF THE WORD

First Reading   *Malachi 3:1*

The Lord says, "I will send my messenger to prepare the way for me." Then the Lord you are looking for will suddenly come to his Temple. The messenger you long to see will come and proclaim my covenant."

This is the Word of the Lord.
  R/. Thanks be to God

Responsorial Psalm

  R/. Who is the King of glory? It is the Lord.

O gates lift up your heads;
Grow higher, ancient doors.
Let him enter, the King of glory!
  R/. Who is the King of glory? It is the Lord.

Who is the King of glory?
The Lord, the mighty, the valiant,
The Lord, the valiant in war.
  R/. Who is the King of glory? It is the Lord.

O gates, lift high your heads;
Grow higher ancient doors.
Let him enter, the King of glory.
  R/. Who is the King of glory? It is the Lord.

Who is he, the King of glory?
He is the Lord of armies,
He is the King of glory.
  R/. Who is the King of glory? It is the Lord.

Second Reading   *Hebrews 2:17-18*

Jesus had to become like his brothers in every way, in order to be their faithful and merciful High Priest in his service to God, so that the people's sins would be forgiven. And now we can help those who are tempted, because he himself was tempted and suffered.

This is the Word of the Lord.
  R/. Thanks be to God.

Gospel Acclamation

Sung

Alleluia, Alleluia!
You are the light of the world.
Alleluia.

Gospel

Luke 2:22-40

The time came for Joseph and Mary to perform the ceremony of purification, as the Law of Moses commanded. So they took the child to Jerusalem to present him to the Lord. At that time there was a man named Simeon living in Jerusalem. He was a good, God-fearing man and was waiting for Israel to be saved. The Holy Spirit was with him and he assured him that he would not die before he had seen the promised Messiah. Led by the Spirit, Simeon went into the Temple. When the parents brought the child Jesus into the Temple to do for him what the Law required, Simeon took the child in his arms and gave thanks to God:

"Now, Lord, you have kept your promise.
And you may let your servant go in peace.
With my own eyes I have seen your
   salvation,
Which you prepared in the presence of all
   peoples:
A light to reveal your will to the Gentiles
And bring glory to your people Israel."

The child's father and mother were amazed at the things Simeon said about him. There was a very old prophetess, a widow named Anna. She never left the Temple; day and night she worshipped God, fasting and praying. That very same hour she arrived and gave thanks to God and spoke about the child to all who were waiting for God to set Jerusalem free.

This is the Gospel of the Lord.
R/. Praise to you, Lord Jesus Christ.

Prayer of the Faithful

[Celebrant] Saving God, with Mary and Joseph we present ourselves to you and we pray for your light.
R/. Open our eyes to your presence.

For all parents and teachers.
R/. Open our eyes to your presence.

For all who long to know you.
R/. Open our eyes to your presence.

For all separated from loved ones.
R/. Open our eyes to your presence.

For all who will die today.
R/. Open our eyes to your presence.

[Celebrant] Light of the world, hear our prayers. May we never walk in darkness, but always seek you. For you are God for ever and ever.
R/. Amen.

■ LITURGY OF THE EUCHARIST

Preparation of the Altar and procession with the Gifts

Music

Prayer over the Gifts

Lord, accept our gifts as we remember your presentation in the Temple. May we recognise your presence in this sacrament of light and love.
We ask this through Christ our Lord
   R/. Amen.

Eucharistic Prayer
Children I

Prayer after Communion

Lord, you fulfilled the hope of Simeon to welcome the Messiah. May this communion prepare us to meet Christ when he comes to bring us to himself.
We ask this in the name of Jesus the Lord.
   R/. Amen.

■ CONCLUDING RITES

Blessing

Dismissal

Recessional hymn
"Shine Jesus Shine"
[Celebration Hymnal for Everyone no.388]

21

SEASONS

2 TEACHER'S NOTES

Background

THIS FEAST is from "Mass of the Candles" since they are blessed and carried in procession this day. Candles are widely used in worship.

They were originally, of course, to allow people to see in the dark. Later they were given the symbolism of light, Christ being the Light of the World.

There are several points to this feast.

It is the feast of the Presentation of the Lord. It commemorates the purification of Mary (a Jewish celebration). We can also see it as a feast of the Holy Family. It celebrates also the beauty of old age in Simeon and Anna

Central focus

The light of Christ in the world. There are five key figures, all little people, the poor that would not be seen as of any account: Mary, Joseph, a baby, and old man and woman, Simeon and Anna.

Offertory

Procession with symbols and gifts:
- ○ Candles.
- ○ Bible as Light of Christ.
- ○ Crib figures (that will be carried off at the end of Mass).

Eucharistic prayer

What is poor and simple, just bread and wine, become in God's hands the wonder of Calvary and Easter commemorated on our altars.

Holy, holy	*Sung*
Memorial acclamation	*Sung*
Great Amen	*Sung*
Communion	*Music*

Follow up

- ○ Taking away crib figures in boxes.
- ○ Using a candle for school prayer or assembly.

3 CELEBRANT'S NOTES

Background

INTRODUCTION TO MASS

CANDLEMAS is the final feast of the Christmas season being the fortieth day. It was celebrated in Jerusalem as early as the fourth century, coming to Europe about a century and a half later. It was originally called "The Purification of Mary" but in recent decades it is seen as a feast of the Lord, his "Presentation in the Temple."

The Jewish ceremony was partly an offering of Jesus to God. We can only guess at the profound meaning of this for Mary and Joseph. The meaning of the feast is largely given by the elderly Simeon and Anna.

Readings

The three readings, here abbreviated, give us the promise of the Lord's coming to his Temple (Malachi), his full sharing in our humanness (Hebrews) and the event itself with the interpretation of Simeon and Anna.

Homily pointers

A new vision:
- ○ The meaning of light.
- ○ The role of older people; they often have the deepest faith.
- ○ Mary and Joseph as simple worshippers.
- ○ Mary and Joseph obeying the Law like everybody else.
- ○ Jesus the Light of the world.
- ○ Finding the light of Jesus.

Communion reflection

Jesus you are my light.
Open my eyes to see you.
Teach me about Mary and Joseph.
Teach me respect for those who are old.

Dismissal

A parting thought: Light and sight are such great gifts.

[Thanks to those who prepared the liturgy and participated in it.]

LENT

1 LITURGY

Opening hymn

Come back to me with all your heart.
Don't let fear keep us apart.
Trees do bend, though straight and tall;
So must we to others call.

Long have I waited for your
coming home to me
And living deeply our new life.

[Celebration Hymnal for Everyone no.122]

© 1972 The Benedictine Foundation of the State of Vermont.

■ INTRODUCTORY RITES

Greeting

Penitential Rite

Lord Jesus, you invite us to love you more deeply.
R/. Lord have mercy.

Lord Jesus, you call us to turn to you always.
R/. Christ have mercy.

Lord Jesus, you offer us compassion and forgiveness.
R/. Lord have mercy.

Opening prayer

Loving God, draw us back to you during this Lenten season. Deepen our love for you each day. We ask this through Jesus Christ our Lord who lives and reigns with you in the unity of the Holy Spirit, one God for ever and ever.
R/. Amen.

■ LITURGY OF THE WORD

First Reading   *Deut. 26:16-19*

Today the Lord your God commands you to obey all his laws; so obey them faithfully with all your heart. Today you have acknowledged the Lord as your God; you have promised to obey him and to do all that he commands. Today the Lord has accepted you as his own people as he promised; you are to obey all his laws. He will make you greater than any other nation that he has created and you will bring praise and honour to his name. You will be his own people, as he promised.

This is the Word of the Lord.
R/. Thanks be to God

Responsorial Psalm   *Psalm 142*

R/. Lord, I cry to you for help.

I call to the Lord for help;
I plead with him.
I bring all my complaints;
When I am ready to give up
He knows what I should do.

R/. Lord, I cry to you for help

In the paths where I walk
My enemies have hidden a trap for me,
When I look beside me I see that there is
no one to help.
No one cares for me.

R/. Lord, I cry to you for help.

Save me from my enemies;
They are too strong for me.
Set me free from my distress;
Then in the assembly of your people
I will praise you because of your goodness to
me.

R/. Lord, I cry to you for help.

Gospel Acclamation   *Sung*

Now, now – it is the Lord who speaks –
Come back to me with all your heart.

Gospel   *Luke 6:36-38*

Jesus said to his disciples: "Be merciful just as
your Father is merciful. Do not judge others, and
God will not judge you; do not condemn others,
and God will not condemn you; forgive others,
and God will forgive you. Give to others, and
God will give to you. Indeed, you will receive a
full measure, a generous helping, poured into
your hands – all that you can hold. The measure
you use for others is the one that God will use
for you."

This is the Gospel of the Lord.

   R/. Praise to you Lord Jesus Christ.

Prayer of the Faithful

[Celebrant] Merciful Father, you call us to
   greater love and repentance. For this grace
   we pray;
   R/. Hear us, merciful Father.

That all leaders in our Church and world will
   work for peace and justice.
   R/. Hear us, merciful Father.

That this school community will draw closer to
   you during this Lenten season.
   R/. Hear us, merciful Father.

That we may forgive as you forgive us.
   R/. Hear us, merciful Father.

That through the prayers of Mary our Mother
   we may reach out to the needy.
   R/. Hear us, merciful Father.

[Celebrant] God of compassion and love hear
   our prayers and journey with us through
   Lent that we may discover its deepest
   meaning.
   We ask this through Jesus our Lord.
   R/. Amen.

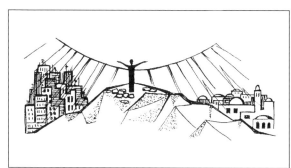

▪ LITURGY OF THE EUCHARIST

Preparation of the Altar and procession with the Gifts   *Music*

Prayer over the Gifts

Lord, bless these gifts and our good
intentions for Lent.
We ask this through Christ our Lord.
   R/. Amen.

Eucharistic Prayer
Reconciliation I

Prayer after Communion

Lord of mercy and love, we thank you for
nourishing us with the Body and Blood of
Jesus. Help us to live the Good News.
We ask this in the name of Jesus the Lord.
   R/. Amen.

▪ CONCLUDING RITES

Blessing

Dismissal

Recessional hymn

"God forgave my sin"

[Celebration Hymnal for Everyone no.209]

SEASONS

2 TEACHER'S NOTES

Background

THE FORTY DAYS of Lent, from Ash Wednesday to Holy Saturday, are a period traditionally for prayer, fasting and doing special good works. The number forty comes from the Lord's fast recorded in the Gospels. An earlier generation associated Lent with giving up things like sweets or some luxuries. The key question is to make Lent meaningful, so that we undertake to do, or give up something, for the whole period. If we do not set down something special and be content with, "I shall be good during Lent," nothing much is likely to result. We also need to look at conversion. Where do I fail, in what areas do I need to be more generous, where do I need the Lord's healing love?

Central focus

The colour of Lent is purple indicating penance. At Lent we all admit our imperfections and our need of God's mercy. It is a time for repentance, for the Sacrament of Reconciliation, and for increased prayer for ourselves and others. Some people will try to attend Mass, visit a Church or say special prayers during this Holy Season.

Offertory

Procession with symbols and gifts:
- ○ Names of school charities to be supported during Lent.
- ○ Sealed envelopes with personal resolutions.
- ○ CAFOD posters.
- ○ Purple drape.
- ○ Poster or banner with Lenten themes, e.g. "Repent", "Come back to Me," "Pray at all times," "People in need" etc.
- ○ Bread and wine – a poor offering, but one made rich by the power of the Spirit.

Eucharistic prayer

Humanity was reconciled to God in the death and resurrection of Jesus – the Paschal Mystery. We commemorate these saving events in each Mass.

Holy, holy	*Sung*
Memorial Acclamation	*Sung*
Great Amen	*Sung*
Communion	*Music*

Follow up

The theme of reconciliation at home and in school; forgiveness; attention to those who are poor or disadvantaged.

3 CELEBRANT'S NOTES

Background

INTRODUCTION TO MASS

LENT became established as a forty-day preparation before Easter about the time of Nicea (325 CE). Forty in the bible means a long time, the number of days recalls the Lord's long fast, forty days (see Matt 4:2; Luke 4:2). Lent was in the early Church the final preparation for baptism; it is still the intensive period of the RCIA programme. The key ideas of Lent are penance and conversion. It could be observed that the element of challenge and generosity have gone from Lent. We are so concerned with being positive, that the real values of giving up things and saying "no" to ourselves have been lost. We are too self-indulgent.

Readings

The Old Testament reading invites us to consider God's Law, which is not an imposition or a test, but it shows us the way we should live so as to be content in ourselves and to do good to others. The New Testament points to one of the crucial virtues, namely mercy.

Homily pointers

Be reconciled to God (see: 2 Cor 5:20):
- ○ Eucharist sacrament of reconciliation.
- ○ We are taught by the Word at Mass and healed through Communion.
- ○ Finding ways of doing penance.
- ○ Showing mercy to others.
- ○ Seeking ways of love.
- ○ Paying special attention to the teaching of Jesus.
- ○ Increasing the quantity and improving the quality of our daily prayer.
- ○ Praying at odd moments of the day.

Communion reflection

In these days of Lent show me Jesus
how you want me to be better.
Jesus give me your strength and grace
to be good.
Jesus teach me to pray.
Jesus bless those who are in need.

Dismissal

Parting thought: Pray always.

[Thanks to those who prepared the liturgy and participated in it.]

EASTER

1 LITURGY

Opening hymn

Thine be the glory,
risen conquering Son
endless is the victory
thou o'er death hast won;
angels in bright raiment
rolled the stone away,
kept the folded grave-clothes,
where thy body lay.

Thine be the glory,
risen conquering Son
endless is the victory
thou o'er death hast won.

[Celebration Hymnal for Everyone no.728]

■ INTRODUCTORY RITES

Greeting

Penitential Rite

Lord Jesus, you free us to live in newness of
life.
R/. Lord have mercy.

Lord Jesus, you heal our brokenness.
R/. Christ have mercy.

Lord Jesus, you are our risen Saviour.
R/. Lord have mercy.

Gloria

Opening prayer

Loving God, as we celebrate the miracle of
the resurrection of Jesus, may we share with
each other the joy and wonder of Easter.
Who lives and reigns with you and the Holy
Spirit, one God, for ever and ever.
R/. Amen.

■ LITURGY OF THE WORD

First Reading
Acts 10:40-43

Peter proclaimed, "God raised him from death
three days later and caused him to appear, not
to everyone, but only to the witnesses that God
had already chosen, that is, to us who ate and
drank with him after he rose from death. And he
commanded us to preach the Gospel to the
people and to testify that he is the one whom
God has appointed judge of the living and the
dead. All the prophets spoke about him, saying
that everyone who believes in him will have his
sins forgiven through the power of his name."

This is the Word of the Lord.
R/. Thanks be to God.

Responsorial Psalm
Psalm 117

*R/. Alleluia, Alleluia,
give thanks to the risen Lord.
Alleluia, alleluia,
give praise to his name.*

Alleluia, alleluia, give praise to his name.
Praise the Lord all you nations!
Praise him, all peoples!
*R/. Alleluia, Alleluia, give thanks to
the risen Lord.
Alleluia, alleluia,
give praise to his name.*

Alleluia, alleluia, give praise to his name.
His love for us is strong
And his faithfulness is eternal.
*R/. Alleluia, Alleluia,
give thanks to the risen Lord.
Alleluia, alleluia,
give praise to his name.*

Gospel Acclamation
Sung

Alleluia, Alleluia, Alleluia!
The Lord has truly risen.
Alleluia, Alleluia, Alleluia!

Gospel   *John 20:11-18*

Mary stood crying outside the tomb. While she was still crying, she bent over and looked in the tomb and saw two angels there dressed in white, sitting where the body of Jesus had been, one at the head and the other at the feet. "Woman why are you crying?" they asked her. She answered, "They have taken my Lord away, and I do not know where they have put him!" Then she turned round and saw Jesus standing there; but she did not know that it was Jesus. Jesus said to her, "Mary! Go to my brothers and tell them that I am returning to him who is my Father and their Father, my God and their God." So Mary Magdalene went and told the disciples that she had seen the Lord and related to them what he had told her.

This is the Gospel of the Lord.

R/. Praise to you, Lord Jesus Christ.

Prayer of the Faithful

[Celebrant] Most loving God, this is the day that you have made, in joy and gratitude we pray:

R/. Risen Lord, stay with us on our journey.

That the Church and all its members will hear your words "Peace be with you".

R/. Risen Lord, stay with us on our journey.

That with your new life we may conquer our sins and addictions.

R/. Risen Lord, stay with us on our journey.

That all who are in prison will hear your good news.

R/. Risen Lord, stay with us on our journey.

That all who die will be welcomed into glory with your words, "Do not be afraid".

R/. Risen Lord, stay with us on our journey.

That we may recognise your presence among us.

R/. Risen Lord, stay with us on our journey.

[Celebrant] Generous God, listen to our prayers and help us to believe and trust in your loving promises.
We ask this in Jesus' name.

R/. Amen.

◼ LITURGY OF THE EUCHARIST

Preparation of the Altar and procession with the Gifts   *Music*

Prayer over the Gifts

Kindly Father, accept these gifts from your family. May we rejoice in the new life you offer us and lead us to eternal life.
We ask this through Christ our Lord.

Eucharistic Prayer Children III

During the Easter Season

Prayer after Communion

Father, look on us with kindness and by these Easter mysteries strengthen us to proclaim your glad tidings.
We ask this in the name of Jesus the Lord.

R/. Amen.

◼ CONCLUDING RITES

Blessing

Dismissal

Recessional hymn

"Alleluia, Alleluia, give thanks to the risen Lord.
Alleluia, alleluia, give praise to his name."

[Celebration Hymnal for Everyone no.32]

SEASONS

2 TEACHER'S NOTES

Background

THE CENTRAL mystery of the Christian faith is the resurrection. Jesus is risen, otherwise our faith would be useless (see 1 Cor 15:1-3.14). Calvary and Easter comprise the Paschal Mystery, they cannot be separated. The resurrection gives meaning to our life and our death; we share his victory over sin and ultimately death. The witnesses of the resurrection were the women who travelled with Jesus and the apostles. The apostles were slow to believe.

The symbols of Easter point to new life: buds and flowers, lambs, eggs. People who recover from illness or addiction are also symbols of life.

Central focus

The death of Jesus led to life for all.
The seed dies to come to life. We all have to lose and give up things so that we can find real riches. The Mass is always a celebration of the Paschal Mystery in which we leave sin and find new life.

Offertory

Procession with symbols and gifts:
- ○ Image of Risen Lord – poster or white drape on a wooden cross.
- ○ Spring flowers and plants.
- ○ Eggs.
- ○ Images of lambs.
- ○ Posters with the word "Life."
- ○ Bread and wine to be changed into the Body and Blood of the Risen Lord.

Eucharistic prayer

We give thanks for life, joy, new hope and good news that come to us from the Cross and resurrection of Jesus.

Holy, Holy	*Sung*
Memorial Acclamation	*Sung*
Great Amen	*Sung*
Communion	*Music*

Follow up

Pay attention to all signs of new life: babies, plants, people's lives.

3 CELEBRANT'S NOTES

Background

INTRODUCTION TO MASS

THE OLDEST and most solemn celebration of the Church's year is Easter, which is continued over a period of forty days, called the Paschal Season.

The two most powerful symbols of Easter are the paschal candle and the often repeated Alleluia, a cry of joy and victory. The great St Augustine taught "We are an Easter people and alleluia is our song."

Easter was also the time when baptism was administered. The new Christians kept celebrating the new life they had received.

All of us are baptised into the death and resurrection of Jesus (see: Rom 6:3-4). It is then the period to celebrate our Christian life and identity.

Readings

The first reading shows a characteristic sermon of the early Church, which proclaims that Jesus is risen. The Gospel tells of the appearance to Mary, one of the women who accompanied Jesus in his ministry.

Homily pointers

Jesus is Risen:
- ❍ A central truth of faith.
- ❍ The source of our baptism.
- ❍ Our life and hope.
- ❍ Victory over death.
- ❍ The great Good News for the world.
- ❍ Acclamations at Mass: "Christ has died, Christ is risen, Christ will come again."
- ❍ Alleluia.

Communion reflection

Jesus, thank you for my baptism.
Jesus, thank you for your forgiveness.
Jesus, keep your way and your truth
 before me.
Jesus, I want to live with you and for you.

Dismissal

Parting thought: "We are an Easter people and alleluia is our song."

[Thanks to those who prepared the liturgy and participated in it.]

ASCENSION

1 LITURGY

Opening hymn

Back to my Father, soon I shall go.
Do not forget me; then you will see
I am still with you, and you will know
You're very close to me.

Filled with my Spirit, how you will grow!
You are my branches; I am the tree.
If you are faithful, others will know.
You are alive in me.

[Celebration Hymnal for Everyone no.730]

© 1978 Bud John Songs / Alliance Media Ltd.. Administered by Copycare.

■ INTRODUCTORY RITES

Greeting

Penitential Rite

Lord Jesus, you call us to forgive and to walk
 in freedom.
 R/. Lord have mercy.

Lord Jesus, you came to heal and save us
 R/. Christ have mercy.

Lord Jesus, you raise us up to greater love
 R/. Lord have mercy.

Gloria   *Sung*

Opening prayer

God of all ages, your glory fills our universe.
Make us joyful in the ascension of your Son
Jesus as we remember his promise: "I will be
with you always."
We ask this through the same Jesus Christ
our Lord who lives and reigns with you and
the Holy Spirit, one God, for ever and ever.
 R/. Amen.

■ LITURGY OF THE WORD

First Reading   *Acts 1:2 -11*

Before he was taken up, he gave instructions by
the power of the Holy Spirit to the men he had
chosen as his apostles. For forty days after his
death he appeared to them many times in ways
that proved beyond doubt that he was alive.
They saw him, and he talked with them about
the Kingdom of God. And when they came
together, he gave them this order: "Do not leave
Jerusalem, but wait for the gift I told you about,
the gift my Father promised. John baptised with
water, but in a few days you will be baptised
with the Holy Spirit." When the apostles met
together with Jesus, they asked him, "Lord, will
you at this time give the Kingdom back to Israel?
Jesus said to them, "The times and occasions
are set by my Father's own authority, and it is
not for you to know when they will be. But when
the Holy Spirit comes upon you, you will be filled
with power, and you will be witnesses for me in
Jerusalem. In all Judaea and Samaria, and to
the ends of the earth." After saying this, he was
taken up to heaven as they watched him, and a
cloud hid him from their sight. They still had
their eyes fixed on the sky as he went away,
when two men dressed in white suddenly stood
beside them and said, "Galileans, why are you
standing there looking up at the sky? This Jesus,
who was taken from you into heaven will come
back in the same way that you saw him go to
heaven."

This is the Word of the Lord.
 R/. Thanks be to God.

Responsorial Psalm   *Psalm 47*

R/. Christ is taken up in glory.

Clap your hands for joy, all peoples!
Praise God with loud songs!
The Lord, the Most High, is to be feared;
He is a great King, ruling over all the world.
R/. Christ is taken up in glory.

God goes up to his throne.
There are shouts of joy and the blast of
    trumpets,
As the Lord goes up.
Sing praise to God;
Sing praise to our King!
God is King over all the world; praise him
    with songs!

R/. Christ is taken up in glory.

Gospel Acclamation   *Sung*

Alleluia, Alleluia!
Go and tell all people my Gospel;
I am with you always until the end of time.
Alleluia.

Gospel   *Mark 16:15-20*

Jesus said to them, "Go throughout the whole
world and preach the Gospel to all. Whoever
believes and is baptised will be saved; whoever
does not believe will be condemned. Believers
will be given the power to perform miracles:
they will drive out demons in my name; they will
speak in strange tongues; if they pick up snakes
or drink any poison, they will not be harmed;
they will place their hands on sick people, who
will get well." After the Lord Jesus had talked
with them, he was taken up to heaven and sat
at the right hand of God. The disciples went and
preached everywhere, and the Lord worked with
them and proved that their preaching was true
by the miracles that were performed.

This is the Gospel of the Lord.

R/. Praise to you, Lord Jesus Christ.

Prayer of the Faithful

[Celebrant] Confident that God calls us to
    celebrate our faith in actions and in words
    we pray:

R/. Be with us always.

That all Christians will spread your message
    with courage.

R/. Be with us always.

That Church and world leaders will work for
    peace and harmony.

R/. Be with us always.

That all victims of war and violence will be
    supported.

R/. Be with us always.

That we may see your presence in this place
    and in all we meet.

R/. Be with us always.

That through the prayers of Mary our Mother
    we may receive your word and act upon it.

R/. Be with us always.

[Celebrant] Faithful God, you revealed yourself
    to us in Jesus. Through the power of your
    Spirit hear our prayers and abide with us.
    We ask this through Jesus our ascended
    Lord.

R/. Amen.

■ LITURGY OF THE EUCHARIST

Preparation of the Altar and procession with the Gifts   *Music*

Prayer over the Gifts

Lord, receive our offerings as we celebrate
the ascension of Christ your Son. May they
please you and help us to rise with him to
the joys of heaven.
We ask this through Christ our Lord.

R/. Amen.

Eucharistic prayer

Preface of the Ascension
Eucharistic Prayer for Children's Masses

Prayer after Communion

Lord, in this Eucharist we touch the divine
life you offer us and all people.
Help us to follow you in love and peace.
We ask this in the name of Jesus the Lord.

R/. Amen.

▥ CONCLUDING RITES

Blessing

Dismissal

Recessional hymn

"New praise be given to Christ newly crowned."

[Celebration Hymnal for Everyone no.508.]

② TEACHER'S NOTES

Background

PAINTINGS of the Ascension usually depict Jesus with his feet in clouds as he goes up to heaven. This can obscure the real meaning of this event for us. The Ascension celebrates Jesus' final departure from his disciples.
It is, however, also the celebration of the mission he has left to his Church.
The final words of a person are always recalled; we recall Jesus' final words to his Church which are a solemn sending to the world with the Good News.

Central focus

Mass is celebrated with Jesus in heaven and with us. It is his offering to the Father, which he allows us to make with him.

Readings

Both readings describe the event of the ascension. Both have the mission or sending of the Church to the world by Jesus. The reading in Acts also tells us about the promised gift of the Holy Spirit. The Gospel speaks of the mission of preaching and healing.

Offertory

Procession with symbols and gifts:
- ❍ Globe/atlas or map of the world.
- ❍ A bridge symbolising heaven and earth joined by Eucharist.
- ❍ Words of Jesus, "I am with you always."
- ❍ Bread and wine.

Eucharistic prayer

The Preface of the Ascension invites us to give thanks because Jesus has gone before us into glory.

Eucharistic prayer for Children's Masses III for Easter season.

Sanctus Acclamation	*Sung*
Memorial Acclamation	*Sung*
Great Amen	*Sung*
Communion	*Sung*

Follow up

Think on what is my mission?
How can I be a good ambassador for Jesus in home and parish?

3 CELEBRANT'S NOTES

Background

INTRODUCTION TO THE MASS

THE EASTER season is rounded off with two big feasts: the Ascension, which celebrates the departure of Jesus and Pentecost, which is his sending of the Holy Spirit. The scriptures tells us about what was on Jesus' mind as he said goodbye to his disciples.

Readings

The first reading is from the Acts of the Apostles, which begins the story of the Church with the departure of Jesus. The Gospel of Mark shows the end of Jesus' life on earth. The ascension is therefore an ending and a beginning.

Homily pointers

The Ascension is counted among the Glorious mysteries of the Rosary; it is not a sad occasion because:
○ Through his ascension "Jesus is Lord" (see 1 Cor 12:3)
○ He has gone to prepare a place for us.
○ He promises the Holy Spirit.
○ He sends the Church on mission.
○ He promises to be always with his Church.
○ He leaves his gift of peace (see John 14:27-28).

Communion reflection

Jesus is always with us.
He is thinking about us; do we think about him?

Dismissal

Parting thought: To allow Jesus to be Lord in our life situations.

[Thanks to those who prepared the liturgy and joined in it.]

CORPUS CHRISTI

1 LITURGY

Opening hymn

This is my Body, broken for you,
Bringing you wholeness, making you free.
Take it and eat it, and when you do,
Do it in love from me.

This is my blood, poured out for you,
Bringing forgiveness, making you free.
Take it and drink it, and when you do,
Do it in love for me.

[Celebration Hymnal for Everyone no.730]

© *1978 Bud John Songs / Alliance Media Ltd. Administered by Copycare*

■ INTRODUCTORY RITES

Greeting

Penitential Rite

Lord Jesus, you are our living bread.

R/. Lord have mercy.

Lord Jesus, you give us the gift of your Body and Blood.

R/. Christ have mercy.

Lord Jesus, you feed us at your table and sustain us on our journey.

R/. Lord have mercy.

Gloria

Opening prayer

Father, your Son, our Lord Jesus, gave us the Eucharist as a memorial of his suffering and death. May we who share in the one bread and drink of the one cup be filled with thankfulness.
We ask this through the same Jesus Christ our Lord, who lives and reigns with you and the Holy Spirit, one God, for ever and ever.

R/. Amen.

■ LITURGY OF THE WORD

First Reading

Gen. 14:18-20

Melchizedek, who was a king of Salem and also a priest of the Most High God, brought bread and wine to Abram, blessed him, and said, "May the Most High God who made heaven and earth, bless Abram! May the Most High God who gave you victory over your enemies, be praised!" And Abram gave Melchizedek a tenth of all the loot he had recovered.

This is the Word of the Lord.

R/. Thanks be to God.

Responsorial Psalm

Psalm 116

R/. I will take the cup of salvation and call on the name of the Lord.

I love the Lord, because he hears me;
He listens to my prayers.
He listens to me every time I call on him.

R/. I will take the cup of salvation and call on the name of the Lord.

What shall I offer to the Lord for all his goodness to me?
I will bring a wine offering to the Lord, to thank him for saving me.

R/. I will take the cup of salvation and call on the name of the Lord.

I will give you a sacrifice of thanksgiving and offer my prayer to you.
In the assembly of all your people,
In the sanctuary of your Temple in Jerusalem
I will give you what I promised.

R/. I will take the cup of salvation and call on the name of the Lord.

Second Reading
1 Cor. 11:23-26

For I received from the Lord the teaching that I passed on to you: that the Lord Jesus, on the night he was betrayed, took a piece of bread, gave thanks to God, broke it, and said, "This is my body, which is for you. Do this in memory of me." In the same way, after the supper he took the cup and said, "This cup is God's new covenant, sealed with my blood. Whenever you drink it, do so in memory of me."
This is the Word of the Lord.

R/. Thanks be to God.

Gospel Acclamation
Sung

Alleluia, Alleluia!
I am the living bread from heaven,
   says the Lord,
whoever eats this bread will live forever.
Alleluia.

Gospel
Mark 14:12-16, 22-26

On the first day of the Festival of Unleavened Bread, the day the lambs for the Passover meal were killed, Jesus' disciples asked him, "Where do you want us to go and get the Passover meal ready for you?" Then Jesus sent two of them with these instructions: "Go into the city, and a man carrying a jar of water will meet you. Follow him to the house he enters, and say to the owner of the house: 'The Teacher says, Where is the room where my disciples and I will eat the Passover meal?' Then he will show you a large upstairs room, prepared and furnished, where you will get everything ready for us." The disciples left, went to the city, and found everything just as Jesus had told them; and they prepared the Passover meal. While they were eating, Jesus took a piece of bread, gave a prayer of thanks, broke it, and gave it to his disciples. "Take it," he said, "This is my body." Then he took a cup, gave thanks to God, and handed it to them; and they all drank from it. Jesus said, "This is my blood which is poured out for many, my blood which seals God's covenant. I tell you, I will never again drink this wine until the day I drink the new wine in the Kingdom of God." Then they sang a hymn and went out to the Mount of Olives.
This is the Gospel of the Lord.

R/. Praise to you, Lord Jesus Christ.

Prayer of the Faithful

[Celebrant] Generous God, you feed us with the bread of your word, hear us as we pray:

R/. Living Lord hear us.

That the Church may manifest Christ in all its actions.

R/. Living Lord hear us.

That we would truly appreciate the gift of the Body and Blood of the Lord.

R/. Living Lord hear us.

That all who have lost loved ones, especially their children, will be comforted.

R/. Living Lord hear us.

That we grow closer to you through the Eucharist.

R/. Living Lord hear us.

That all who have lapsed may know your love and mercy.

R/. Living Lord hear us.

[Celebrant] God of life, your love is beyond understanding. Listen to our prayers spoken and unspoken and continue to help us in our need.
We ask this through Christ our Lord.

R/. Amen.

SEASONS

■ LITURGY OF THE EUCHARIST

Preparation of the Altar and procession with the Gifts   *Music*

Prayer over the Gifts

Lord may this offering of our love be acceptable to you. Let it transform our lives and bring us your peace and mercy.
We ask this through Christ our Lord.

R/. Amen.

Eucharistic Prayer

Preface of Corpus Christi
Eucharistic Prayer for Children's Masses

Prayer after Communion

Lord, you give us your body and blood in the Eucharist as a sign that even now we share your life. Draw us closer to you and help us to recognise you in all we meet.
We ask this in the name of Jesus the Lord.

R/. Amen.

■ CONCLUDING RITES

Blessing

Dismissal

Recessional hymn

"Lord Jesus you have come to us"

[Celebration Hymnal for Everyone no.383]

2 TEACHER'S NOTES

Background

THE CHURCH has a feast of the Body of the Lord (Latin: *Corpus Christi*) which invites us to consider and give thanks for the greatest gift God has given us in his Son Jesus Christ. The Second Vatican Council (1962-1965) and the Synod of Bishops in 2005 spoke of the Eucharist being the "source and summit of the whole Christian life."

Central focus

The Eucharist is spiritual food for our journey; it is also where the word is broken and our faith is enriched.

Readings

Since Corpus Christi is one of the greatest feasts, there are three readings.
The first is a distant foreshadowing of the Eucharist in the sacrificial offering of the priest Melchizedek perhaps 1600 years before Christ.
The second reading is how St Paul handed on the central teaching about Jesus giving us the Blessed Eucharist.
The Gospel shows us the context which is the Last Supper, the final meal of Jesus with his apostles.

Offertory

Procession with symbols and gifts:
- ○ Grapes.
- ○ Food for the needy.
- ○ Money for CAFOD or similar charity.
- ○ Names of those making First Communion in the school.
- ○ Bread and wine.

Eucharistic Prayer For Children III

The "Preface of the Holy Eucharist II" gives in a very brief space why we should today thank God: for the gift of the Body and Blood of the Lord, for his food, for his strength, for the grace it gives.

Sanctus Acclamation	*Sung*
Memorial Acclamation	*Sung*
Great Amen	*Sung*
Communion	*Music*

Follow up

When we visit a church, Jesus is there waiting to hear from us; we can speak our desires, our hopes, our fears, our needs.

2 CELEBRANT'S NOTES

Background

INTRODUCTION TO THE MASS

THE EUCHARIST means thanksgiving. For over a thousand years the Church has had a feast of Corpus Christi (Latin: "Body of Christ").

The feast with its readings and prayers helps us to appreciate more deeply the wonderful gift that Jesus has given to his Church.

The Eucharist is the sacrifice of the Church; it is a sacramental meal which feeds us; it is the Blessed Sacrament since Jesus is present in our tabernacles to be adored and to comfort us.

Readings

The Genesis reading about the shadowy priest Melchizedek points to the Eucharist being a sacrifice, prefigured in an offering of bread and wine in the time of Abraham about 1650 years before Christ. Paul hands on to the Corinthians what he himself was taught about the Last Supper. He reminds us that it is a covenant offering, that is, it is the bond that unites God with his people. The Gospel reading is an account of the Passover meal of the Last Supper.

Homily pointers

Various aspects of the great mystery can be considered (see Catechism of the Catholic Church nn. 1322-1419, esp. 1328-1332):

- ❍ The two tables at which we are fed at Mass: the word that teaches, the supper that feeds us.
- ❍ Holy Communion.
- ❍ The Mass as sacrifice.
- ❍ A memorial meal that Jesus celebrates with us.
- ❍ The Blessed Sacrament through which Jesus remains with his Church.
- ❍ The centre of the life of the Church.

Communion reflection

Let us tell Jesus what is in our hearts.

Dismissal

To remember as we pass a Catholic church that Jesus is there. A reverent "Hi Lord," a whispered prayer, a sign of the Cross as we go by; if the church is open, we could drop in for a simple visit to Jesus so that he might bless us and listen to how we are today.

PENTECOST

1 LITURGY

Opening hymn

Abba, Father send your Spirit.
Glory, Jesus Christ *(2)*
Glory, hallelujah, glory, Jesus Christ! *(2)*

[Celebration Hymnal for Everyone no.8]

© Shalom Community

▪ INTRODUCTORY RITES

Greeting

Penitential Rite

Lord Jesus, you send us your Spirit of Peace.
R/. Lord have mercy.

Lord Jesus, you send us your Spirit of Hope.
R/. Christ have mercy.

Lord Jesus, you send us your Spirit of
Forgiveness.
R/. Lord have mercy.

Gloria

Opening prayer

God our Father, let the Spirit you sent on the
Church to begin the teaching of the Gospel
continue to work in the lives of all who
believe in you.
We ask this through Jesus Christ our Lord
who lives and reigns with you and the Holy
Spirit, one God, for ever and ever.
R/. Amen.

▪ LITURGY OF THE WORD

First Reading

Acts 2:1-11

When the day of Pentecost came, all the
believers were gathered together in one place.
Suddenly there was a noise from the sky which
sounded like a strong wind blowing, and it filled
the whole house where they were sitting. Then
they saw what looked like tongues of fire which
spread out and touched each person there. They
were all filled with the Holy Spirit and began to
talk in other languages, as the Spirit enabled
them to speak. There were Jews living in
Jerusalem, religious men who had come from
every country in the world. When they heard
this noise, a large crowd gathered. They were all
excited, because each one of them heard the
believers speaking in his own language. In
amazement and wonder they exclaimed, "These
people who are talking like they are Galileans!
How is it, then, that all of us hear them in our
own native languages? We are from Parthia,
Media, and Elam; from Mesopotamia, Judaea,
and Cappadocia; from Pontius and Asia, from
Phrygia and Pamphylia, from Egypt and the
regions of Libya near Cyrene. Some of us are
from Rome, both Jews and Gentiles converted to
Judaism, and some of us are from Crete and
Arabia – yet all of us hear them speaking in our
own languages about the great things that God
has done!"

This is the Word of the Lord.
R/. Thanks be to God.

Responsorial psalm

Psalm 105

R/. Send us your Spirit, Lord.

Give thanks to the Lord,
Proclaim his greatness;
Tell the nations what he has done
Sing praise to the Lord;
Tell of the wonderful things he has done.
R/. Send us your Spirit, Lord.

The Lord is our God;
His commands are for all the world.
He will keep his covenant forever,
His promises for a thousand generations.

R/. Send us your Spirit, Lord.

He opened a rock, and water gushed out,
Flowing through the desert like a river,
He remembered his sacred promise
To Abraham his servant.

R/. Send us your Spirit, Lord.

Second Reading
Gall. 5:22-25

The Spirit produces love, joy, peace patience, kindness, goodness, faithfulness, humility and self-control. There is no law against such things as these. And those who belong to Christ Jesus have put to death their human nature with all its passions and desires. The Spirit has given us life; he must also control our lives.

This is the word of the Lord.

R/. Thanks be to God.

Gospel acclamation

Alleluia, Alleluia!
Come, Holy Spirit,
fill the hearts of your faithful
and kindle in them the fire of your love.
Alleluia.

Gospel
John 15:26-27; 16:12-15

"The Helper will come – the Spirit, who reveals the truth about God and who comes from the Father. I will send him to you from the Father, and he will speak about me. And you, too, will speak about me, because you have been with me from the beginning. I have much more to tell you, but now it would be too much for you to bear. When, however, the Spirit comes, who reveals the truth about God, he will lead you into all truth. He will not speak on his own authority, but he will speak of what he hears, and will tell you of things to come. He will give me glory, because he will take what I say and tell it to you. All that my Father has is mine; that is why I said that the Spirit will take what I give him and tell it to you."

This is the Gospel of the Lord.

R/. Praise to you, Lord Jesus Christ.

Creed

Prayer of the Faithful

[Celebrant] We turn to our great God and pray in confidence.

R/. Come, Holy Spirit.

That the leaders of the Church will be filled with your Spirit and new vision.

R/. Come, Holy Spirit.

That all nations and people will be open to your gift of peace.

R/. Come, Holy Spirit.

That all who are sad will receive your gift of joy.

R/. Come, Holy Spirit.

That through the prayers of Mary, our mother we will be filled with a new zeal for your kingdom.

R/. Come, Holy Spirit.

[Celebrant] Creator of all, you stirred the apostles to go out and proclaim the Good News; hear our prayers and help us to work for a more loving world.
Through Christ our Lord.

R/. Amen.

■ LITURGY OF THE EUCHARIST

Preparation of the Altar and procession with the gifts
Music

Prayer over the Gifts

Lord, may the Spirit you promised us lead us into all truth and teach us the full meaning of this Eucharist.
We ask this through Christ our Lord.

R/. Amen.

SEASONS

Eucharistic Prayer

Eucharistic Prayer for Children b) "God guides the Church on the Way of Salvation."
or
For Children III "During the Easter Season" with Preface of the Holy Spirit.

Prayer after Communion

Lord you give us the Body and Blood of your Son to know your life within us.
In your mercy, assure our redemption and bring us to the eternal life we celebrate in this Eucharist.
We ask this in the name of Jesus the Lord.

R/. Amen.

■ CONCLUDING RITES

Blessing (Solemn)

Bow your heads and pray for God's blessing.
(This day) the Father of light has enlightened the minds of the disciples by the outpouring of the Holy Spirit.
May he bless you and give the gifts of the Spirit for ever.

R/. Amen.

May that fire which hovered over the disciples as tongues of flame burn out all evil from your hearts and make them glow with pure light.

R/. Amen.

God inspired speech in different tongues to proclaim our faith. May he strengthen your faith and fulfil your hope of seeing him face to face.

R/. Amen.

May almighty God bless you, the Father, and the Son, and the Holy Spirit.

R/. Amen.

Dismissal

Recessional hymn

"Holy Spirit of Fire"

Celebration Hymnal for Everyone, no.262

2 TEACHER'S NOTES

Background

BIRTHDAYS are important; today we celebrate the birthday of the Church. Jesus had promised the Holy Spirit. On the fiftieth (Gk. *pentêkostê*) day after Easter he came with power on the Church gathered around Mary in prayer.
From being frightened and hiding, the apostles became bold witnesses to Christ.

Central focus

The Holy Spirit comes at each Mass to change the bread and wine into the Body and Blood of Jesus. He also comes upon all those gathered at Mass to give the gift of unity and love.

Readings

The three readings tell us about the Holy Spirit. The Gospel shows us Jesus promising to send the Holy Spirit after his departure through Calvary, Easter and the Ascension.
The first reading from Acts describes the coming of the Spirit in tongues. The second brief reading shows us the fruit of the Spirit, how we should live and what are to be our attitudes towards God, towards other people and towards ourselves.

Offertory

Procession with symbols and gifts:
- ◯ Symbols of the Spirit: dove, flames.
- ◯ Picture of Pentecost.
- ◯ Banner with gifts of the Spirit (wisdom, understanding, right judgement, strength, knowledge, reverence, wonder and awe).
- ◯ Banner with fruit of the Spirit (love, joy, peace patience, kindness, goodness, faithfulness, humility and self-control).
- ◯ Banner with names of those confirmed recently from school.
- ◯ Bread and wine.

Eucharistic Prayer

Eucharistic Prayer for Children III
"During the Easter Season"
with Preface of the Holy Spirit I or II.

The Preface always tells us why today we give thanks at Mass, which is the gift, love and guidance of the Holy Spirit.

Acclamation	*Sung*
Memorial Acclamation	*Sung*
Great Amen	*Sung*
Communion	*Music*

Follow up

Over the next few weeks remind pupils about one of the gifts or fruit of the Holy Spirit.

3 CELEBRANT'S NOTES

Background

INTRODUCTION TO THE MASS

THERE was a time when the Holy Spirit was almost forgotten. We can easily identify with Father, and Son, but Spirit is more difficult.

In Hebrew Spirit, *Ruah*, is feminine, in Greek *pneuma* is neuter, and in Latin *Spiritus* is masculine. We come to learn about, and know the Holy Spirit by seeing how he touches the life of the Church. In the rite of confirmation he is called "Helper and Guide;" In the Creed he is called "Lord and Giver of Life."

The Church must always live by the Spirit. So we gather to learn about the Holy Spirit in the first part of the Mass, and then to give thanks for his gifts to the Church and us.

Readings

The three readings tell us about the Holy Spirit. The first reading described the dramatic coming of the Spirit in fire and tongues. The second text tells us about the fruit of the Spirit that should be present in our lives. The Gospel is Jesus' promise to send the Holy Spirit.

Homily pointers

The homily might indicate some of the works of the Holy Spirit in the Church:

❍ In each one of the sacraments, it is the Spirit who gives grace.

❍ In the Eucharist changing the bread and wine into the Body and Blood of the Lord, and gathering the congregation into one. Every Mass invokes the Spirit on the gifts and on the Church.

❍ In our lives giving us the gifts we need to be followers of Christ: for every situation there is one of the Confirmation gifts at our disposal, if we ask.

❍ The Spirit as "Helper and Guide" as "Lord and Giver of Life" or as our "Friend" (name given by St Thomas Aquinas d. 1274).

❍ Develop gifts of the Spirit (wisdom, understanding, right judgement, strength, knowledge, reverence, wonder and awe).

❍ Develop fruit of the Spirit (love, joy, peace patience, kindness, goodness, faithfulness, humility and self-control).

Communion reflection

Ask Jesus to send us his Holy Spirit: "Come Holy Spirit".

Dismissal

Remember that we can always turn to our Helper and Guide, to our Friend, the Holy Spirit.

[Thanks to those who prepared the liturgy and participated in it.]

MASS OF OUR LADY

1 LITURGY

Opening hymn

"Holy Virgin, by God's decree"

[Celebration Hymnal for Everyone no.263]

■ INTRODUCTORY RITES

Greeting

Penitential Rite

You offer us your word.

R/. Lord have mercy.

You invite us to trust and hope.

R/. Christ have mercy.

You encourage us to do your will.

R/. Lord have mercy.

Opening prayer

God our Father, your eternal Son became man and was born of the Virgin Mary. Through her prayers deepen our love for you. We ask this in his name, for he is Lord for ever and ever.

R/. Amen.

■ LITURGY OF THE WORD

First Reading

Ephesians 1:3-6,11-12

Let us give thanks to the God and Father of our Lord Jesus Christ! For in our union with Christ he has blessed us by giving us every spiritual blessing in the heavenly world. Even before the world was made, God had already chosen us to be his through our union with Christ, so that we would be holy and without fault before him.

This is the Word of the Lord.

R/. Thanks be to God

Responsorial Psalm

Songs of the Spirit 1, no.72

R/. My soul proclaims the greatness of the Lord.

My soul proclaims the Lord my God.
My spirit sings his praise!
He looks on me, he lifts me up,
and gladness fills my days.

R/. My soul proclaims the greatness of the Lord.

All nations now will share my joy,
his gifts he has out-poured;
his little ones he has made great;
I magnify the Lord.

R/. My soul proclaims the greatness of the Lord.

His mercy is for evermore!
His name I praise again!
His strong right arm puts down the proud
and raises lowly men!

> R/. *My soul proclaims the greatness
> of the Lord.*

He fills the hungry with good things,
the rich he sends away.
The promise made to Abraham
is filled by him each day.

> R/. *My soul proclaims the greatness
> of the Lord.*

Gospel Acclamation   *Sung*

Alleluia, alleluia, alleluia!
The Lord has done great things for me.
Alleluia.

Gospel   *Matthew 12:46-50*

Jesus was still talking to the people when his mother and brothers arrived. They stood outside, asking to speak with him. So one of the people there said to him, "Look, your mother and brothers are standing outside, and they want to speak with you." Jesus answered, "Who is my mother? Who are my brothers?" Then he pointed to his disciples and said, "Look! Here are my mother and my brothers! Whoever does what my Father in heaven wants him to do is my brother, my sister, and my mother."

This is the Gospel of the Lord.

> R/. *Praise to you, Lord Jesus Christ.*

Prayer of the Faithful

[Celebrant] Almighty God, you gave us Mary as the model of holiness through her intercession we pray.

> R/. *Your will be done, O Lord.*

That all Christians will trust in God's promises.

> R/. *Your will be done, O Lord.*

That we will listen to God's Word.

> R/. *Your will be done, O Lord.*

That all mothers will be loved and respected.

> R/. *Your will be done, O Lord.*

[Celebrant] Father in heaven, listen to our prayers which we make invoking the intercession of Mary, through your Son, and in his name, for he is Lord for ever and ever.

> R/. *Amen.*

■ LITURGY OF THE EUCHARIST

Preparation of the Altar and procession with the Gifts   *Music*

Prayer over the Gifts

Lord, we offer these gifts which bring us peace and joy. Increase our love for you and for each other.
We ask this through Christ our Lord.

> R/. *Amen.*

Eucharistic Prayer
Children I

Prayer after Communion

Lord, you chose Mary our Mother and kept her free from sin. May this sacrament make us strong and keep us faithful to you.
We ask this in the name of Jesus the Lord.

> R/. *Amen.*

■ CONCLUDING RITES

Blessing

Dismissal

Recessional hymn

O lady, full of God's own grace,
whose caring hands the child embraced,
who listened to the Spirit's word,
believed and trusted in the Lord.

O virgin fair, star of the sea,
my dearest mother, pray for me.

[Celebration Hymnal for Everyone no.538]

45

FEASTS

2 TEACHER'S NOTES

Background

THE STORY of our salvation, cannot be told without remembering Mary, Mother of Jesus. We say in the Creed on Sundays: "Through the power of the Holy Spirit he became incarnate of the Virgin Mary and was made man." God became a member of our human race to save us by having a human Mother, Mary of Nazareth. The Creator God made her lovely, preparing a Mother for his Son. She had many graces to make her completely holy. She said a full "yes" to God's plan at the Annunciation. She had to follow out this plan right up to seeing her Son die on Calvary.

Central focus

Mary is always to be found with Jesus her Son. We honour her because of him. A good son will always be happy to see his mother praised and appreciated.

Readings

The first reading outlines God's great plan for salvation, which is centred on the death and glorification of Jesus and the sending of the Holy Spirit on the Church.
The Gospel looks at an incident in the public ministry of Jesus, which indicates that the relationship Jesus wanted from everybody, including his Mother, is that of doing the will of his Father in heaven.

Offertory

Procession with symbols and gifts:
- ❍ Picture of the Blessed Virgin Mary.
- ❍ Flowers and one candle to honour this image.
- ❍ Banner with the words, "Hail Mary."
- ❍ Bread and wine that will become the Body and Blood of Jesus.

Eucharistic Prayer

We note that in every Eucharistic Prayer the Church recalls that the community is worshipping the Trinity along with the Virgin Mary, the angels and saints.

Holy, holy	*Sung*
Memorial acclamation	*Sung*
Great Amen	*Sung*
Communion	*Music*

Follow up

Leave an image of the Blessed Virgin in the classroom or assembly hall during the following week with some flowers. Light candles for common worship. During this time share some reflections on the meaning of the *Hail Mary*.

3 CELEBRANT'S NOTES

Background

INTRODUCTION TO THE MASS

FROM very early times the Church has honoured Mary. It was she who allowed God to be born as man in Jesus Christ. We cannot speak of Incarnation without remembering Mary: the Mother at Bethlehem, at Nazareth, at Calvary. Catholics honour Mary as God's masterpiece out of all humanity; she is also one of us who knows the pain of human living and our needs.

Readings

The Letter to the Ephesians begins with a great sweep of history from eternity to our present time and reaching out to the end of time. God is at work in Jesus Christ and through the Holy Spirit. The Gospel gives us a surprising little incident from the life of Jesus: what is he saying to his Mother and to us?

Homily pointers

Some contrasts which are ideas that we must hold together, not choosing one only:

○ Mary as the greatest in the Church, but closest to us (see Vatican II, *Church* LG 51).
○ Mary is Mother of Jesus, but she is also Mother of his Body the Church; Mother therefore of Head and members of the Body.
○ Jesus loves his Mother, but appreciates obedience to his Father's will above all else.
○ We worship God, but we can also honour Mary.
○ It is only Jesus who saves, but we can ask Mary's help in preparing us to receive his grace.

Communion reflection

There is a little prayer ascribed to St Ignatius Loyola (d. 1556), who founded the Jesuit order:

"Mary, show me your Son;
Jesus show me your Mother."

Dismissal

During this day we can think over some phrases of the Hail Mary...

ALL SAINTS [1 November]

1 LITURGY

Opening hymn

> Oh when the saints go marching in,
> Oh when the saints go marching in,
> I want to be in that number,
> When the saints go marching in.
>
> *[Celebration Hymnal for Everyone no.571]*

■ INTRODUCTORY RITES

Greeting

Penitential Rite

Lord Jesus, you call us to lead good lives.
> *R/. Lord have mercy.*

Lord Jesus, you call us out of darkness into your light.
> *R/. Christ have mercy.*

Lord Jesus, you are the Resurrection and the life.
> *R/. Lord have mercy.*

Gloria

Opening prayer

> Father of life we rejoice in the holy men and women of all ages and places.
> May we be filled with the Spirit that marked their lives and strive to live in peace and love.
> We ask this through our Lord Jesus Christ, your Son, who lives and reigns with you and the Holy Spirit, one God, for ever and ever.
> > *R/. Amen.*

■ LITURGY OF THE WORD

First Reading — *Revelation 7:2.4.9.12*

And I saw another angel coming up from the east with the seal of the living God. And I was told that the number of those who were marked with God's seal on their foreheads was 144,000. They were from the twelve tribes of Israel. After this I looked, and there was an enormous crowd – no one could count all the people! They were from every race, tribe, nation, and language, and they stood in front of the throne and of the lamb, dressed in white robes and holding palm branches in their hands. They called out in a loud voice: "Salvation comes from our God who sits on the throne, and from the Lamb!" All the angels stood round the throne, the elders and the four living creatures. Then they threw themselves face downwards in front of the throne and worshipped God, saying, "Amen! Praise, glory, wisdom, thanksgiving, honour, power, and might belong to our God forever and ever! Amen!"

This is the Word of the Lord.
> *R/. Thanks be to God.*

Responsorial Psalm — *Psalm 24*

> *R/. Who is the great King?,*
> > *he is the Lord the strong and mighty.*

> The world and all that is in it
> > belong to the Lord;
> The earth and all who live on it are his.
> He built it on the deep waters
> > beneath the earth
> And laid its foundations in the ocean depths.

> *R/. Who is the great King?,*
> > *he is the Lord the strong and mighty.*

> Who has the right to go up the Lord's hill?
> Who may enter his holy temple?
> Those who are pure in act and thought,
> Who do not worship idols or make false promises.

> *R/. Who is the great King?,*
> > *he is the Lord the strong and mighty.*

The Lord will bless them and save them;
God will declare them innocent.
Such are the people who come to God,
Who come into the presence of the God
   of Jacob.

R/. *Who is the great King?,*
   he is the Lord the strong and mighty.

Second Reading
1 John 3:1-3

See how much the Father has loved us! His love is so great that we are called God's children – and so, in fact, we are. This is why the world does not know us: it has not known God. My dear friends we are now God's children, but it is not yet clear what we shall become. But we know that when Christ appears, we shall be like him, because we shall see him as he really is. Everyone who has this hope in Christ keeps themselves pure, just as Christ is pure.

This is the Word of the Lord.

R/. *Thanks be to God.*

Gospel Acclamation
Sung

Alleluia, Alleluia!
I am the Way, the Truth and the Life
   says the Lord.
Alleluia!

Gospel
Matthew 5:1-2

Jesus saw the crowds and went up a hill, where he sat down. His disciples gathered round him, and he began to teach them:

"Happy are those who know they are
   spiritually poor;
      the Kingdom of heaven belongs to them!

Happy are those who mourn;
   God will comfort them!

Happy are those who are humble;
   They will receive what God has
      promised!

Happy are those whose greatest desire is to
do what God requires;
   God will satisfy them fully!

Happy are those who are merciful to others;
   God will be merciful to them!

Happy are the pure in heart;
   They will see God!

Happy are those who are persecuted because they do what God requires;
   The Kingdom of heaven belongs to them!

Happy are you when people insult you and persecute you and tell all kinds of evil lies against you because you are my followers.
   Be happy and glad, for a great reward is kept for you in heaven!

This is how the prophets who lived before you were persecuted."

This is the Gospel of the Lord.

R/. *Praise to you, Lord Jesus Christ.*

Creed

Prayer of the Faithful

[Celebrant] Like a shepherd, the Lord continues to care for us, so we pray with confidence:

R/. *Saints in glory praise our God.*

That all who are baptised may enter the company of the saints.

R/. *Saints in glory praise our God.*

That people of all nations will work for harmony and peace.

R/. *Saints in glory praise our God.*

That all who are seriously ill will be comforted.

R/. *Saints in glory praise our God.*

That all our loved ones who have died will join your saints in glory.

R/. *Saints in glory praise our God.*

That we learn to serve you through the witness of the lives of the saints.

R/. *Saints in glory praise our God.*

[Celebrant] God of heaven and earth you reward those with clean hands and pure hearts: in our unworthiness listen to our prayers. Through Christ our Lord.

R/. *Amen*

LITURGY OF THE EUCHARIST

Preparation of the Altar and procession with the Gifts   *Music*

Prayer over Gifts

Lord, we are united in this sacrament by the love of Christ. Accept these gifts and bring us to share with our brothers and sisters already in glory.
We ask this through Christ Our Lord.
R/. Amen.

Eucharistic Prayer

Masses for Children II

Prayer after Communion

Father and Source of all good we praise your glory reflected in the saints.
May we who share at this altar be filled with your love and be prepared for the joy of your Kingdom, where Jesus is Lord for ever and ever.
R/. Amen.

Solemn Blessing

Bow your heads and pray for God's blessing.

God is the glory and joy of all his saints,
Whose memory we celebrate today.
May his blessing be with you always.
R/. Amen.
May the prayers of the saints deliver you from
    present evil;
May their example of holy living
Turn your thoughts to the service of God and
    neighbour.
R/. Amen.
God's holy Church rejoices that her children
Are one with the saints in lasting peace.
May you come to share with them
In all the joys of our Father's house.
R/. Amen.
May almighty God bless you,
The Father, and the Son, and the Holy Spirit.
R/. Amen.

Dismissal

Recessional hymn   "For all the Saints"

[Celebration Hymnal for Everyone no.176]

50

2 TEACHER'S NOTES

Background

A HOLY DAY to honour all the saints in a common feast. In the 'Apostles Creed' we confess our belief in the communion of saints. Communion here is a sharing; the word 'saints' here can mean either holy persons or holy things. So it is a feast of sharing. We celebrate all the holy people who are now with God. They are like a friendly crowd cheering on a team. We are the players, with the saints wanting us to win. The great saints are a model and inspiration; they are teachers about how to live the Christian life; they are our friends.

In the East since the fourth century a feast honoured the martyrs; it was later enlarged to include non-martyrs. In the West the saints and martyrs were honoured with a feast from the early seventh century.

Central focus

The whole of the Church, living and dead, takes part in the Eucharist. We always say in the Eucharistic prayer that we are praying with Mary and all the saints (see Vatican II, *Liturgy* SC 8).

Readings

Since it is a solemnity, there are three readings supplied for this day. For school Masses one might choose either the Revelation reading which looks at the saints in glory, or the reading from John which tells us about the love of God which drew the saints along in life until they reached glory. The Gospel text shows the path for all: the Beatitudes taught by Jesus in his Sermon on the Mountain.

Offertory

Procession with symbols and gifts

- ❍ Books about saints.
- ❍ Differing sizes of footprints as all follow Jesus in different ways.
- ❍ Some pictures of saints or sayings of saints.
- ❍ Bread and wine which will be changed into heavenly food and drink.

Eucharistic Prayer

In the Eucharistic prayer we should note the references to Mary and the Saints, as well as the prayer for the deceased.

Holy Holy	*Sung*
Memorial acclamation	*Sung*
Great Amen	*Sung*
Communion	*Music*

Follow up

In the days/weeks ahead pupils should gather material on the patron of the school, on the patron of the parish. They could be taught the meaning of statues, icons and pictures which help to remind us of the saints and to focus our own prayer.

3 CELEBRANT'S NOTES

Background

INTRODUCTION TO MASS

WHAT DO we mean by saints? They are holy people. But what does it mean to be holy. It means to be seized by God, surrounded by divine love and brought to God. Sometimes we see a dog that is dragged along on the lead. The image of the saints is more people who walk along with God at the pace that he sets for them and in the direction that he wants them to travel.

Readings

There are three readings supplied for this day. The reading from Revelation is a graphic picture of all the saints in glory. The second reading supplied shows how the saints came to glory: they were drawn by God's love. The Gospel shows the way to holiness, the beatitudes taught by Jesus.

Homily pointers

- ❍ Being saints
- ❍ Everyone is called to be holy.
- ❍ There are many ways to holiness.
- ❍ We are meant to be holy now, not when we grow up.
- ❍ The path to holiness is the beatitudes, that is the attitudes and patterns of living taught by Jesus.
- ❍ Holiness is not so much deciding what things to do, but rather of surrendering to God's love. Holiness is more a response than an initiative.
- ❍ Examples from the life of Our Lady or the school patron.

Communion reflection

Jesus I thank you for coming to me.
Make me open to accept your love.
I want to be holy to please you and help others.
Show me how to be loving at home and school.

Dismissal

A parting thought: When you see the picture of a saint, stop and think for a moment.

[Thanks to those who prepared the liturgy and participated in it.]

REMEMBRANCE

1 LITURGY

Opening hymn

Amazing grace! How sweet the sound
That saved a wretch like me.
I once was lost, but now I'm found, was
blind, but now I see.

[Celebration Hymnal for Everyone no.40]

■ INTRODUCTORY RITES

Greeting

Penitential Rite

Lord Jesus, you raised the dead to life.

R/. Lord have mercy.

Lord Jesus, you showed compassion for all who
were sad.

R/. Christ have mercy.

Lord Jesus, you healed the broken-hearted.

R/. Lord have mercy.

Opening prayer

God, our Creator and Redeemer, Christ your
Son conquered death and returned to you in
glory. Hear our prayer for all our loved ones,
whom we raise up to you now, that they may
see your face forever.
We ask this through our Lord Jesus Christ,
your Son, who lives and reigns with you and
the Holy Spirit, one God, for ever and ever.

R/. Amen.

■ LITURGY OF THE WORD

First Reading   *Revelation 21:4-5; 22:4-5*

God himself will be with them and he will be
their God. He will wipe away all tears from their
eyes, there will be no more death, no more grief
or crying or pain. The old things have
disappeared. They will see his face, and his
name will be written on their foreheads. There
shall be no more night, and they will not need
lamps or sunlight, because the Lord God will be
their light, and they will rule as kings forever
and ever.

This is the Word of the Lord.

R/. Thanks be to God.

Responsorial Psalm   *Psalm 27*

R/. The Lord is my light and my help.

The Lord is my light and my salvation;
I will fear no one.
The Lord protects me from all danger;
I will never be afraid.

R/. The Lord is my light and my help.

I have asked the Lord for one thing;
One thing only do I want:
To live in the Lord's house all my life,
And to marvel there at his goodness.

R/. The Lord is my light and my help.

I know that I will live to see the Lord's
goodness
In this present life.
Trust in the Lord. Have faith, Do not despair.
Trust in the Lord.

R/. The Lord is my light and my help.

Gospel Acclamation   *Sung*

Alleluia, Alleluia!
Come to me all you who are burdened
and I will give you rest.
Alleluia!

Gospel
John 6:37-40

[Jesus said:] Everyone whom my Father gives me will come to me. I will never turn away anyone who comes to me, because I have come down from heaven to do not my own will but the will of him who sent me. And it is the will of him who sent me that I should not lose any of all those he has given to me, but that I should raise them all to life on the last day. For what my Father wants is that all who see the Son and believe in him should have eternal life. And I will raise them to life on the last day.

This is the Gospel of the Lord.

R/. Praise to you, Lord Jesus Christ.

Prayer of the Faithful

[Celebrant] Living God, you raised Jesus from the dead and promised us new life through his resurrection. With faith in your promise we pray:

R/. Lord in your mercy, hear our prayer.

That all who have died will enjoy the fullness of your presence.

R/. Lord in your mercy, hear our prayer.

That the Church may gain inspiration from the past.

R/. Lord in your mercy, hear our prayer.

That all who mourn at this time will be comforted.

R/. Lord in your mercy, hear our prayer.

That all who care for the sick and dying will show compassion and love.

R/. Lord in your mercy, hear our prayer.

That we may be grateful for the love we have received from people who have passed to the Lord.

R/. Lord in your mercy, hear our prayer.

[Celebrant] Hear and grant our prayers we make to you through Christ our Lord.

R/. Amen.

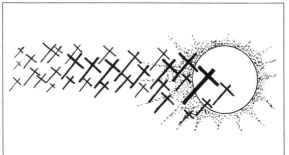

■ LITURGY OF THE EUCHARIST

Preparation of the Altar and procession with the Gifts
Music

Prayer over the Gifts

Lord, we are united in this sacrament by the love of Christ. Accept these gifts and receive our brothers and sisters into the glory of your Son, who is Lord for ever and ever.

R/. Amen.

Eucharistic prayer
Children III, outside Easter

Prayer after Communion

Lord God, may the death and resurrection of Christ which we celebrate in this Eucharist bring all who have died to the peace of your eternal love.
We ask this in the name of Jesus the Lord.

R/. Amen.

■ CONCLUDING RITES

Blessing

Dismissal

Recessional hymn

"You shall cross the barren desert".

[Celebration Hymnal for Everyone no.830]

2 TEACHER'S NOTES

Background

NOVEMBER is the month of remembrance. In the Catholic Church there is the celebration of All Souls, when we remember our dead friends and relatives, and indeed all the dead. The Church commends them all to the Lord's mercy and we give thanks for all that we have received through them.

It is also a time of national remembrance when those who have died for our country are remembered and those who have given their lives for peacekeeping, abroad. The British symbol of remembrance is the poppy (*genus papaver*) which grew profusely in Flanders where so many died during the First World War (1914-1918).

Central focus

The Mass is a meeting place of all God's children in the Communion of Saints. We join with the saints already in glory and we make intercession for the dead who may still need healing by the Lord.

Offertory

Procession with symbols and gifts:
○ Bouquet of flowers or bunch of wild flowers.
○ Placard or banner: "We will remember them."
○ [Poppies for Remembrance Day]
○ A school or class book in which children and teachers have written the names of dead friends and relatives, or those who they once admired and are now dead.
○ Bread and wine which after the Consecration will unite heaven and earth.

Eucharistic Prayer

In the Eucharistic Prayer we unite heaven and earth. We celebrate along with Mary and the saints and pray for the dead.

Sanctus Acclamation	*Sung*
Memorial Acclamation	*Sung*
Great Amen	*Sung*
Communion	*Sung*

Follow up

To learn the prayer of the Church for all the dead:

Eternal rest give to them O Lord,
and let perpetual light shine on them.
Amen.
May they rest in peace.
Amen.

To learn the *Act of Remembrance*:

They shall not grow old,
as we who are left grow old.
Age shall not weary them,
nor the years condemn.
At the going down of the sun
and in the morning
we will remember them.

FEASTS

3 CELEBRANT'S NOTES

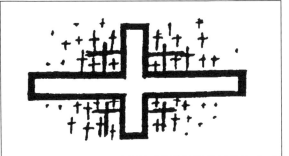

Background

INTRODUCTION TO MASS

CHURCH and State are in remembrance mode in November. Newscasters on TV and many people begin to wear poppies from about the beginning of the month. The poppy is a remembrance of the Flanders' slaughter in the first World War (1914-1918). The Church remembers the dead in the whole month of November. It is good that people place the names of loved ones in the altar list of the dead. The focus of the Mass is the Communion of Saints: Heaven, earth and those being purified for eternal life.

Readings

The first reading looks forward to the time when all will be in glory, when all pain and distress will be finished. The Gospel is a reminder that Jesus came to save all and raise them up on the last day.

Homily pointers

The Communion of Saints:
- ❍ Heaven and earth join in Mass.
- ❍ Those in heaven care for us.
- ❍ Along with the saints, we care for those who have died.
- ❍ The pain and distress that we meet are not permanent: we are on the way home to God.
- ❍ The need to be grateful to those who have died for our country or in peacekeeping missions.
- ❍ Our duty to remember our own dead friends and relatives and to be grateful to them for what they have done for us.

Communion reflection

Jesus, look on my dead friends and relatives:
Tell them that I love them.
Give them peace.
Jesus, I trust in you.

Dismissal

A parting thought: Heaven and earth are close.

[Thanks to those who prepared the liturgy and participated in it.]

OUR LADY OF LOURDES (11 February)

1 LITURGY

Opening hymn

Hail Mary, full of grace,
the Lord is with you.
Blessed are you among women,
and blessed is the fruit of thy womb, Jesus.
Holy Mary, Mother of God, pray for us
   sinners,
now and at the hour of our death. Amen.
Gentle woman, quiet light,
morning star, so strong and bright,
gentle mother, peaceful dove,
teach us wisdom, teach us love.

[Celebration Hymnal for Everyone no.236]

■ INTRODUCTORY RITES

Greeting

Penitential Rite

Lord Jesus, you heal and restore us.
   R/. Lord have mercy.

Lord Jesus, you are the river of life.
   R/. Christ have mercy.

Lord Jesus, you embrace us in a rainbow of
   mercy.
   R/. Lord have mercy.

Opening prayer

Gentle Father, we celebrate this feast of
Mary. May we learn from her the way of
patient waiting, faithful love, compassion for
the suffering and difficulties of others, and to
say with her "Let it be done to me according
to your word."
We ask this through Jesus Christ our Lord
who lives and reigns with you and the Holy
Spirit one God for ever and ever.
   R/. Amen.

■ LITURGY OF THE WORD

First Reading   Isaiah 61:9-11

"They will be famous among the nations;
everyone who sees them will know that they are
a people whom I have blessed." Jerusalem
rejoices because of what the Lord has done. She
is like a bride dressed for her wedding. God has
clothed her with salvation and victory. As surely
as seeds sprout and grow, the Sovereign Lord
will save his people. And all the nations will
praise him.

This is the Word of the Lord.
   R/. Thanks be to God.

Responsorial Psalm   Luke 1:46-55

   *R/. My soul proclaims your greatness,
      O Lord.*

My soul proclaims the Lord my God,
My Spirit sings his praise!
He looks on me, he lifts me up,
And gladness fills my days.

   *R/. My soul proclaims your greatness,
      O Lord.*

All nations now will share my joy,
His gifts he has outpoured;
His little one he has made great;
I magnify the Lord.

   *R/. My soul proclaims your greatness,
      O Lord.*

For those who love his holy name,
His mercy will not die.
His strong right arm puts down the proud
And lifts the lowly high.

   *R/. My soul proclaims your greatness,
      O Lord.*

He fills the hungry with good things,
The rich he sends away.
The promise made to Abraham
Is filled to endless day.

   *R/. My soul proclaims your greatness,
      O Lord.*

Gospel Acclamation *Sung*

Alleluia, Alleluia,
Magnificat, magnificat,
Magnificat, praise God!
Praise God, praise God, praise God,
    praise God,
Magnificat, praise God!
Alleluia.

Gospel *Luke 11:27-28*

When Jesus had said this, a woman spoke up from the crowd and said to him, "How happy is the woman who bore you and nursed you!" But Jesus answered, "Rather, how happy are those who hear the word of God and obey it!"

This is the Gospel of the Lord.

R/. Praise to you Lord Jesus Christ.

Prayer of the Faithful

[Celebrant] Loving God, you have given us Mary as our Mother, too, we pray with her now:

R/. Let your will be done.

That the Church and all its leaders will be blessed.

R/. Let your will be done.

That all who suffer in mind and body will be healed.

R/. Let your will be done.

That all who care for the sick will be rewarded.

R/. Let your will be done.

That all who travel to Lourdes in search of healing will be strengthened.

R/. Let your will be done.

That we may ponder with Mary your blessings in prayer.

R/. Let your will be done.

[Celebrant] Father, listen favourably to our prayers and help us to trust in your mercy and love as Mary did. We ask this through Christ our Lord.

R/. Amen.

■ LITURGY OF THE EUCHARIST

Preparation of the Altar and procession with the Gifts *Music*

Prayer over the Gifts

Lord, accept these gifts we offer in honour of Mary. May we follow her example and grow in holiness and love.
We ask this through Christ our Lord.

R/. Amen.

Eucharistic Prayer Children I

Prayer after Communion

Lord, you nourish us in this sacrament. Through the prayers of Our Lady of Lourdes we ask you to strengthen us that we may lead good lives and live in your love.
We ask this in the name of Jesus the Lord.

R/. Amen.

■ CONCLUDING RITES

Blessing

Dismissal

Recessional hymn

"Immaculate Mary".

[Celebration Hymnal for Everyone no.300]

or

"Holy Virgin by God's decree".

[Celebration Hymnal for Everyone no.263]

FEASTS

2 TEACHER'S NOTES

Background

ON THE 11th February 1858 Our Lady appeared to Bernadette Soubirous. The little French girl did not know at first who the mysterious lady was; later she heard her say, "I am the Immaculate Conception." Lourdes became the greatest place of Catholic pilgrimage in the world, a place where people go seeking healing of mind, soul and body. Pope John Paul II instituted the feast as World Day for the Sick. Lourdes is also a place where the marginalized are welcome, especially in the City of the Poor.

Central focus

We are all in need of healing. Some people are physically sick; many are damaged through others or through the circumstances of life. We all have memories that make us squirm with embarrassment or fear. Well-being means being able to handle sickness and deal with hurtful situations or memories.

The Eucharist is a healing sacrament; at Mass we pray before Communion "Say but the word and I shall be healed."

Offertory

Procession with symbols and gifts:

- ○ Medicine and bandages indicating medical care.
- ○ Candles recalling the Lourdes processions with light.
- ○ Names of those we know are sick at this time.
- ○ Statue or picture of Our Lady.
- ○ Rosary beads indicating one of the great prayers at Lourdes.
- ○ Bread and wine for Mass; they will be the source of healing and strength.

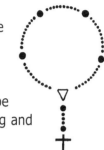

Eucharistic prayer

The main cures at Lourdes usually occur not at the grotto but during the Procession and Benediction with the Blessed Sacrament.

The centre of Lourdes is not Mary, but Jesus whose death and glorification are celebrated in so many Masses, and adored in the exposition Chapel.

Holy, Holy	*Sung*
Memorial Acclamation	*Sung*
Great Amen	*Sung*
Communion	*Music*

Follow up

Continue with class or school prayers for the sick, especially parents, grandparents and other friends and relations of pupils and school staff.

❸ CELEBRANT'S NOTES

Background

INTRODUCTION TO MASS

LOURDES is the greatest pilgrimage centre in Europe. Thousands go there to honour Mary and especially to seek healing. Healing is about having fullness of life (see John 10:10).

A person may be quite ill and still have real life; a person who is quite well physically may be miserable. Many people need healing in their bodies, others in the emotions and memories, others need spiritual healing from the effects of sin. This Mass focuses on praying for the sick as well as being open to whatever healing we may need.

Readings

The reading from Isaiah celebrates the beauty that comes from God. The Gospel shows how we are to adorn our lives, by obeying God's word like Mary.

Homily pointers

Healing:

- ○ Painful memories.
- ○ Hurts of the past.
- ○ Physical sickness.
- ○ Prayer for those who need healing.
- ○ Eucharist as the great healing sacrament: healing mentioned three times at Communion.
- ○ Acceptance of our own weakness.
- ○ Forgiveness to those who have hurt us.

Communion reflection

Jesus, I need your healing to be strong in loving you.
Jesus, help me to be brave in speaking about you.
Jesus, bless people I know are sick
Jesus, show me the beauty of Mary, our Mother.

Dismissal

Parting thought: I can always seek strength and help at Mass.

[Thanks to those who prepared the liturgy and joined in it.]

ST. DAVID

1 LITURGY

Opening hymn

Guide me, O thou great Redeemer,
Pilgrim through this barren land;
I am weak, but thou are mighty,
Hold me with thy pow'rful hand.
Bread of heaven, bread of heaven,
Feed me till I want no more. *(x2)*

Open now the crystal fountain,
Whence the healing stream doth flow;
Let the fire and cloudy pillar
Lead me all my journey through;
Strong Deliverer, Strong Deliverer,
Be thou still my strength and shield. *(x2)*

[Celebration Hymnal for Everyone no.233]

■ INTRODUCTORY RITES

Greeting

Penitential

You call us to live in love.
> *R/. Lord have mercy.*

You invite us to lead good lives.
> *R/. Christ have mercy.*

You offer us freedom and peace.
> *R/. Lord have mercy.*

Opening prayer

Loving God, may the example of St David
make us courageous in following you.
May we be filled with the Spirit that marked
his life.
We ask this through our Lord Jesus Christ,
your Son, who lives and reigns with you and
the Holy Spirit, one God, for ever and ever.
> *R/. Amen.*

■ LITURGY OF THE WORD

First reading
Isaiah 61:1-3

The Lord has filled me with his Spirit. He has
chosen me and sent me to bring good news to
the poor, to heal the broken-hearted, to
announce release to captives and freedom to
those in prison. He has sent me to proclaim that
the time has come when the Lord will save his
people and defeat their enemies. He has sent
me to comfort all who mourn, to give those who
mourn joy and gladness instead of grief, a song
of praise instead of sorrow. They will be like
trees that the Lord has planted. They will all do
what is right, and God will be praised for what
he has done.

This is the Word of the Lord.
> *R/. Thanks be to God.*

Responsorial Psalm
Psalm 63

> *R/. I will sing songs of praise to you.*

O God, you are my God,
and I long for you.
My whole being desires you;
like a dry, worn-out and waterless land
my soul is thirsty for you.
> *R/. I will sing songs of praise to you.*

Your constant love is better than life itself,
and so I will praise you.
I will give you thanks as long as I live:
I will raise my hands to you in prayer.
> *R/. I will sing songs of praise to you.*

Gospel Acclamation
Sung

Alleluia, Alleluia
Here I am, Lord!
I come to do your will.
Alleluia.

Gospel *Matthew 5:14-16*

In the sermon on the Mount, Jesus taught: "You are like light for the whole world. A city built on a hill cannot be hidden. No one lights a lamp and puts it under a bowl; instead it is put on a lamp-stand, where it gives light for everyone in the house. In the same way your light must shine before people, so that they will see the good things you do and praise your Father in heaven."

This is the Gospel of the Lord.

> *R/. Praise to you Lord Jesus Christ.*

Prayer of the faithful

[Celebrant] Gracious God, with St David we raise our hearts in prayer:

> *R/. Show your light to the world.*

We ask your guidance and protection for the Church in Wales.

> *R/. Show your light to the world.*

We ask God's blessing on all who promote and safeguard Welsh culture and language.

> *R/. Show your light to the world.*

We ask that we may follow David in being peacemakers.

> *R/. Show your light to the world.*

We ask you to bless all who have the name David.

> *R/. Show your light to the world.*

[Celebrant] God of all nations listen to our prayers and grant that through the intercession of Mary and St David your light may shine through us.
We make this prayer through Christ our Lord.

> *R/. Amen.*

▪ LITURGY OF THE EUCHARIST

Preparation of the Altar and procession with the Gifts *Music*

Prayer over the Gifts

Lord we are united in this sacrament by the love of Christ. Accept these gifts as we remember the example of St David.
May we recognise your presence of light and love among us.
We ask this through Christ our Lord.

> *R/. Amen.*

Eucharistic Prayer

Eucharistic Prayer for Children I

We give thanks for the ministry of Jesus and we allow him to touch our lives.

Prayer after Communion

Lord, may this sacrament fill us with the same love and zeal as St David.
Strengthen us as we go out to serve you.
We ask this in the name of Jesus the Lord.

> *R/. Amen.*

■ CONCLUDING RITES

Blessing

Dismissal

Recessional hymn

"O great St David".

[Celebration Hymnal for Everyone no.532]

---

2 TEACHER'S NOTES

Background

THE SIXTH century St David is the patron saint of Wales. The Welsh form of the name is Dafydd. He founded several strict monasteries, the principal one being St David's in Pembrokeshire. Monks came from Ireland and all parts of Britain to study under him. He was venerated at the great monastery of Glastonbury. He was bishop of Menevia.

Focus

The wonder and beauty of the saints. Some saints have the power of uniting a whole people or culture. We bring all of our lives to the Mass.

Readings

The first reading reminds us of David's Spirit-filled life which drew people from all parts of these islands. The choice of Gospel hints at the legend that David was miraculously lifted up at an important synod so that he could be seen and heard.

Offertory

Procession with symbols and gifts:
- ❍ Basket of daffodils or leeks.
- ❍ Map of Wales.
- ❍ Symbols of Welsh culture: choirs, music, poetry.
- ❍ Photographs of Welsh Assembly or Festival (Eisteddfod).
- ❍ List of pupils and staff with the name "David."
- ❍ Welsh bible or New Testament.
- ❍ Bread and wine.

Eucharistic Prayer
Eucharistic Prayer for Children I

We give thanks for the ministry of Jesus and allow him to touch our lives.

Acclamation	*Sung*
Memorial Acclamation	*Sung*
Great Amen	*Sung*
Communion	*Music*

Follow up

Bydded I fendwith,	May the blessing of
Duw Dad,	God the Father,
Duw Fab,	God the Son,
Duw Ysbryd Glan,	God the Holy Spirit,
I aros gyda chi o'r amser	Remain with you from this time
Hun hyd yn oes oesoedd	And for ever and ever.
Amen.	Amen.

3 CELEBRANT'S NOTES

Background

INTRODUCTION TO THE MASS

EVEN IN Shakespeare's time there was a custom of Welsh people wearing leeks or daffodils on his feast. But the origin of this practice is unknown. They are still worn today.

The feast of St David is a day of national rejoicing, pride and cultural celebration.

The Church enters into all that is good in national life and hence celebrates a liturgy appropriate for the saint. There is not much known about details of David's life, but his inspiration has been huge during and after his lifetime. He died around AD 600.

Readings

The readings evoke aspects of the memory of David. He was a Spirit-filled man, known for works of love and compassion. The Gospel hints at the time when the ground on which he stood at a synod at Brevi was said to have been raised so that he could be seen and heard.

Homily pointers

The homily can range over the issues of intergration of culture and the Church.

- ○ The Church in Wales celebrates the patron of the country.
- ○ The ancient monastic life of the Celtic countries.
- ○ The memory of the saints persists when kings are forgotten.
- ○ Geoffrey of Monmouth recalled the last word of David in his monastery at Minevia: "Be joyful, brothers and sisters. Keep the faith and do the little things you have heard and seen me do."

Communion reflection

Hear Jesus saying to you:
"Be joyful... keep the faith."

Dismissal

Christians should be proud of their country and pray for its well-being

[Thanks to those who prepared the liturgy and participated in it.]

ST. PATRICK

1 LITURGY

Opening hymn

Christ be beside me, Christ be before me,
Christ be behind me, King of my heart.
Christ be within me, Christ be below me,
Christ be above me, never to part.

Christ on my right hand, Christ on my left hand,
Christ all around me, shield in the strife.
Christ in my sleeping, Christ in my sitting,
Christ in my rising, light of my life.

[Celebration Hymnal for Everyone no.106]

© Geoffrey Chapman (a division of Cassell PLC)

■ INTRODUCTORY RITES

Greeting

Penitential Rite

Lord Jesus, you call us out of selfishness into light.

R/. Lord have mercy.

Lord Jesus, you free us from the slavery of sin.

R/. Christ have mercy.

Lord Jesus, you are close to us always.

R/. Lord have mercy.

Opening prayer

God of boundless love, you sent St Patrick to preach your message of love and peace to the people of Ireland.
By the help of your grace may Christians everywhere proclaim your love.
We ask this through Jesus Christ our Lord, who lives and reigns with you and the Holy Spirit, one God, for ever and ever.

R/. Amen.

■ LITURGY OF THE WORD

First Reading
Jeremiah 1:4-9

The Lord said to me, "I chose you before I gave you life, and before you were born I selected you to be a prophet to the nations." I answered, "Sovereign Lord, I don't know how to speak; I am too young." But the Lord said to me, "Do not say that you are too young, but go to the people I send you to, and tell them everything I command you to say. Do not be afraid of them, for I will be with you to protect you. I, the Lord, have spoken! Then the Lord stretched out his hand, touched my lips, and said to me, "Listen, I am giving you the words you must speak."

This is the Word of the Lord.

R/. Thanks be to God.

Responsorial Psalm
Psalm 27

R/. The Lord is my light and my help.

The Lord is my light and my salvation;
I will fear no one.
The Lord protects me from all danger;
I will never be afraid.

R/. The Lord is my light and my help.

I have asked the Lord for one thing;
One thing only do I want;
To live in the Lord's house all my life,
To marvel there at his goodness.

R/. The Lord is my light and my help.

Don't be angry with me;
Don't turn your servant away.
You have been my help;
Don't leave me, don't abandon me,
O God my Saviour.

R/. The Lord is my light and my help.

Gospel Acclamation

Sung

Glory to you, O Christ you are
the Word of God.
We do not live on bread alone
but on every word that comes from God.
Glory to you, O Christ you are
the Word of God.

Gospel

Luke 10:1-12

After this the Lord chose another seventy-two men and sent them out two by two, to go ahead of him to every town and place where he himself was about to go. He said to them, "There is a large harvest, but few workers to gather it in. Pray to the owner of the harvest that he will send out workers to gather in his harvest. Go! I am sending you like lambs among wolves. Don't take a purse or a beggar's bag or shoes; don't stop to greet anyone on the road. Whenever you go into a house, first say, 'Peace be with this house.' If a peace loving man lives there, let your greeting of peace remain on him; if not, take back your greeting of peace. Stay in that same house, eating and drinking whatever they offer you, for a worker should be given his pay. Don't move round from one house to another. Whenever you go into a town and are made welcome, eat what is set before you, heal the sick in that town, and say to the people there, 'The kingdom of God has come near you!' "

This is the Gospel of the Lord.

R/. Praise to you, Lord Jesus Christ.

Prayer of the Faithful

[Celebrant] God and Father, you sent your Son Jesus to show us the fullness of your love for us, hear our prayer.

R/. Help us answer your call.

That our Pope and Bishops will be inspired by your Holy Spirit.

R/. Help us answer your call.

That all who have wandered away from you will return to your love.

R/. Help us answer your call.

That all Christians will be courageous in spreading your Good News.

R/. Help us answer your call.

That the people of Ireland [*That the Celtic nations†*] will be faithful to St Patrick's message and example.

R/. Help us answer your call.

That all who risk their lives for the Gospel will be supported.

R/. Help us answer your call.

[Celebrant] Faithful God, listen to our prayers and through St Patrick's intercession grant them through Christ our Lord.

R/. Amen.

† Alternative form

▪ LITURGY OF THE EUCHARIST

Preparation of the Altar and procession with the Gifts

Music

Prayer over the Gifts

Father, with selfless love St Patrick followed your call to preach your love to the people of Ireland. Strengthen us to serve you at this altar with pure hearts.
We ask this through Christ our Lord. Amen.

Eucharistic Prayer
Eucharistic Prayer II

Prayer after Communion

Lord, may the sacrament we have received fill us with the same zeal and love as St Patrick. May it help us in this life and in the life to come.
We ask this in the name of Jesus the Lord.

R/. Amen.

■ CONCLUDING RITES

Blessing

Dismissal

Recessional hymn

Christ on my right hand, Christ on my
left hand,
Christ all around me, shield in the strife.
Christ in my sleeping, Christ in my sitting,
Christ in my rising, light of my life.

Christ be in all hearts thinking about me.
Christ be in all tongues telling of me.
Christ be the vision in eyes that see me,
In ears that hear me, Christ ever be.

[Celebration Hymnal for Everyone no.106]

2 TEACHER'S NOTES

Background

THOUGH Irish patron, St Patrick is venerated in many places throughout the world. He was born in Britain, probably Wales. Captured by sea-pirates he was sold as a slave and herded animals on Slemish mountain in the North East of Ireland.
He escaped but in a vision he heard the call of the Irish to return. He returned as a bishop and remained the rest of his life preaching to the Irish whom he found a difficult people. His dates are not certain; he is usually said to have died about 461AD or perhaps somewhat later.

Central focus

The Eucharist is always about the proclamation of the Word. When we are instructed by God, then we are more open to offer ourselves along with Jesus in his sacrifice and to receive him in the sacrament and experience his healing

Offertory

Procession with symbols and gifts:
- ○ Outline map of the British Isles and Ireland showing places associated with the saint.
- ○ Green banner.
- ○ Bible.
- ○ Copy of the *Confession* of St Patrick or a poster with the Breastplate of Patrick.
- ○ Bread and wine: the Mass, though its ceremonial has changed, is the same sacrifice offered by St Patrick.

Eucharistic prayer

The Second Eucharistic Prayer was basically in use before Patrick's time. In the Mass we are in continuity across the centuries.

Holy Holy	*Sung*
Memorial Acclamation	*Sung*
Great Amen	*Sung*
Communion	*Music*

Follow up

Learn the *Breastplate* of Patrick.

Christ be with me, Christ be behind me,
Christ be before me, Christ be beside me,
Christ to win me, Christ to comfort and
restore me,
Christ beneath me, Christ above me,
Christ in quiet, Christ in danger,
Christ in hearts of all that love me,
Christ in mouth of friend and stranger.

3 CELEBRANT'S NOTES

Background

INTRODUCTION TO MASS

ST PATRICK is assuredly venerated by Irish people. We should also see him as a British saint, being probably born in Wales.

Since he appears in the universal Church calendar he belongs to all. In a multicultural society we need to celebrate identities and differencies, but at the same time ensure that these are enrichment and not divisive in a school or parish. The Mass should celebrate what is universal in the message of Patrick. His dates are not certain, but certainly fifth century. His death is variously given as 461 or about 490. The facts of his life are obscured by legend. The key resource is his *Confession*, written late in life to celebrate God's grace working through him. It is one of the great documents of the Church's mystical heritage and shows Patrick in his weakness and in his rugged strength.

Readings

The readings are about calling (Jeremiah) and sending (the seventy-two). Both express the feelings and experience of Patrick as recorded in his *Confession*.

Homily pointers

St Patrick:
- ○ knew weakness and discouragement,
- ○ experienced betrayal by those close to him,
- ○ was treated with cruelty in captivity.
- ○ was always at prayer as he worked with herds on the mountain, or travelled around Ireland,
- ○ kept going,
- ○ never lost faith in God's love and protection,
- ○ gave all the credit for his ministry to God.

Communion reflection

Jesus, thank you for coming to me.
In weakness may I turn to you.
In success may I give you thanks.
May I always be aware that you are close to me.

Dismissal

Parting thought: "Christ be with me"
(from St Patrick's *Breastplate*).

[Thanks to those who prepared the liturgy and participated in it.]

ST. JOSEPH

1 LITURGY

Opening hymn

St Joseph God has chosen you
To keep his Church from harm
So hold the Church as once you held
The Christ-Child in your arms.

[Celebration Hymnal for Everyone no.627]

© *James J. Donahue*

■ INTRODUCTORY RITES

Greeting

Penitential

Lord God, you chose us before the world began.

R/. Lord have mercy.

Lord God, you are our rock of safety.

R/. Christ have mercy.

Lord God, under your watchful care we rest secure.

R/. Lord have mercy.

Opening prayer

Father you entrusted Jesus to the care of St Joseph. By his protection and example may we grow in knowledge and love of you. We ask this through Jesus Christ our Lord who lives and reigns with you in the unity of the Holy Spirit one God for ever and ever.

R/. Amen.

■ LITURGY OF THE WORD

First Reading
Romans 4:13, 16-18, 22

God promised Abraham and his descendants that the world would belong to him because he believed and was accepted as righteous by God. For Abraham is the spiritual father of us all; as the scripture says, "I have made you father of many nations."

R/. Thanks be to God.

Responsorial Psalm
Psalm 89

R/. I know that your love will last for all time.

O Lord I will always sing of your constant love;
I will proclaim your faithfulness forever.
I know that your love will last for all time.

R/. I know that your love will last for all time.

He will say to me,
'You are my father and my God;
You are my protector and my saviour.'
I will make him my first-born son,
The greatest of all kings.

R/. I know that your love will last for all time.

Gospel Acclamation
Sung

Glory to you O Christ.
You are the Word of God.

They are happy who dwell in your house, O Lord.

Glory to you O Christ.
You are the Word of God.

In Eastertide, add Alleluia at beginning and end.

Gospel
Matthew 1:18-21, 24

This was how the birth of Jesus Christ took place. An angel of the Lord appeared to Joseph in a dream and said, "Joseph, descendant of David, do not be afraid to take Mary to be your wife. For it is by the Holy Spirit that she has conceived. She will have a son, and you will name him Jesus – because he will save his people from their sins." So when Joseph woke up, he married Mary, as the angel of the Lord had told him to do. Mary gave birth to her Son, and Joseph named him Jesus.

This is the Gospel of the Lord.

R/. Praise to you, Lord Jesus Christ.

Prayer of the Faithful

[Celebrant] God of mystery, you chose Joseph the just man to be the foster father of Jesus, listen to our prayer which we make with his help:

R/. God of love hear us.

That the Church may be protected through the prayer of St Joseph, its guardian.

R/. God of love hear us.

That families everywhere will know the blessings of love and support from you and other people.

R/. God of love hear us.

That all who find employment difficult will be strengthened.

R/. God of love hear us.

That parents and carers will guide their children wisely.

R/. God of love hear us.

That like Joseph we will obey your Word always.

R/. God of love hear us.

That we may be peace loving and peacemaking.

R/. God of love hear us.

[Celebrant] Ever-loving Father hear our prayer in Jesus' name.

R/. Amen.

■ LITURGY OF THE EUCHARIST

Preparation of the Altar and procession with gifts
Music

Prayer over the Gifts

Father, with generous love St Joseph loved and cared for Jesus. May we also love and support one another.
We ask this through Christ our Lord.

R/. Amen.

Eucharistic Prayer
Jesus the Compassion of God

Prayer after Communion

Lord, you nourish us at this Eucharist; through the prayers of St Joseph protect us in your love.
We ask this in the name of Jesus the Lord.

R/. Amen.

■ CONCLUDING RITES

Blessing

Dismissal

Recessional hymn

"St Joseph was a carpenter"

[A Year of Celebration no.37]

2 TEACHER'S NOTES

Background

JOSEPH was the husband of Mary. He was traditionally said to be a carpenter. He was foster father of Jesus and therefore was responsible with Mary for forming Jesus in the Law, and in religious and social matters. He looked after the Holy Family when they were refugees in Egypt. Since he almost certainly died before the public ministry of Jesus, his death is seen in Christian tradition as ideal: dying in the presence of Jesus and Mary. He is thus patron of a happy death.

Since he cared for these two in his life, he is venerated as Guardian of the Church.

Central focus

Everything about Joseph is simple, yet his role was most important. His simple life roots our thinking about his wife and his adopted son living in a small insignificant village. The Mass too grounds us in worship and in the concrete reality of daily living.

Offertory

Procession with symbols and gifts:
- ○ Some simple tools.
- ○ An angel figure or picture.
- ○ Refugee posters or symbols.
- ○ Bread and wine, the food of Mary and Joseph, are to be changed into the Body and Blood of their Son.

Eucharistic prayer

In the Eucharistic prayer we give thanks for all we have received, especially the good things that have come to us through Jesus Christ.

Holy holy	*Sung*
Memorial Acclamation	*Sung*
Great Amen	*Sung*
Communion	*Music*

Follow up

Various examples of the beauty of simple things.

③ CELEBRANT'S NOTES

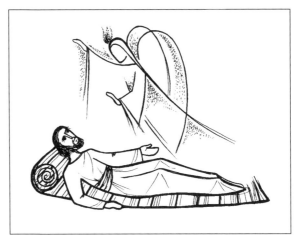

Background

INTRODUCTION TO MASS

LITURGICAL devotion to St Joseph was rather late in the Western Church, a feast established in Rome in fifteenth century. Since in Latin and early forms of French, Italian, etc. the word "family" meant a household, it was only when these languages, including English, used "family" for the restricted unit of parents and their children that devotion to the Holy Family arose in Europe in the sixteenth century. Traditionally he is said to be a carpenter, but the word used in the Gospels may also mean one who works in stone and in wood.

As he almost certainly died before the ministry of Jesus, he is patron of a happy or ideal death – with Jesus and Mary.

Readings

God's plan was from eternity. It began to become concrete in Abraham (see genealogy in Matt 1:1-17). The Gospel shows Joseph being instructed by God's angel as well as his obedience.

Homily pointers

St Joseph:
- ○ Became holy through looking after Jesus and Mary.
- ○ The dignity of work.
- ○ A man of integrity open to be taught by God.
- ○ Life is made up of simple things.
- ○ Keeping close to Mary and to Jesus.
- ○ Protector of the Church.
- ○ Patron of dying.
- ○ Model and teacher of prayer.

Communion reflection

Jesus, Mary and Joseph I give you
my heart and soul.
Jesus, Mary and Joseph teach me
how to live in your way.
Jesus, Mary and Joseph I hope to
live with you forever.

[Traditional prayer]

Dismissal

Parting thought: Talk to Jesus, Mary and Joseph about my family.

[Thanks to those who prepared the liturgy and participated in it.]

ST. GEORGE

1 LITURGY

Opening hymn

O God our help in ages past
Our hope for years to come,
Our shelter from the stormy blast,
And our eternal home.

Beneath the shadow of thy throne,
Thy saints have dwelt secure;
Sufficient is thine arm alone,
And our defence is sure.

O God our help in ages past
Our hope for years to come,
Be thou our guard while troubles last,
And our eternal home.

[Celebration Hymnal for Everyone, no.528]

■ INTRODUCTORY RITES

Greeting

Penitential Rite

You laid down your life for us.
   R/. Lord have mercy.

You encourage us when we weaken.
   R/. Christ have mercy.

You are our way, our truth, and life.
   R/. Lord have mercy.

Opening prayer

Merciful God, may the witness of St George,
soldier and martyr, encourage us to live lives
of peace, love and justice.
We ask this through our Lord Jesus Christ,
your Son, who lives and reigns with you and
the Holy Spirit, one God, for ever and ever.
   R/. Amen.

■ LITURGY OF THE WORD

First Reading   *Romans 12:9-21 (extracts)*

Love must be completely sincere. Hate what is
evil, hold on to what is good. Serve the Lord
with a heart full of devotion. Be happy with
those who are happy, weep with those who
weep. Have the same concern for everybody. If
someone has done you wrong, do not repay with
wrong. Do everything possible to live in peace
with everybody. Never take revenge. Do not let
evil defeat you, instead conquer evil with good.

This is the Word of the Lord.
   R/. Thanks be to God.

Responsorial Psalm   *Psalm 33*

   R/. May your constant love be with us, Lord.

Happy the nation whose God is the Lord
Happy are the people he has chosen for his
   own.
   R/. May your constant love be with us, Lord.

A king does not win because of his powerful
   army;
A soldier does not triumph because of his
   strength.
   R/. May your constant love be with us, Lord.

May your constant love be upon us, Lord
as we put our hope in you.
   R/. May your constant love be with us, Lord

Gospel Acclamation   *Sung*

Alleluia! Alleluia!
Your Kingdom Lord is truth and life.
Alleluia! Alleluia!

Gospel
Luke 9:23

Jesus said to them all, "If anyone wants to come with me they must forget self, take up their cross and follow me.

This is the Gospel of the Lord.

R/. *Praise to you, Lord Jesus Christ.*

Prayer of the Faithful

[Celebrant] God of all nations and armies confident that you will help us to overcome evil we pray:

R/. *Lord, protect and guide us.*

That the Church may be bold in proclaiming Christ.

R/. *Lord, protect and guide us.*

That the Royal Family may be examples for all.

R/. *Lord, protect and guide us.*

That all peoples will live in harmony and peace.

R/. *Lord, protect and guide us.*

That we may love our country and respect all its citizens.

R/. *Lord, protect and guide us.*

That we may recognise the evil and sin in our lives and in society, and try to overcome it.

R/. *Lord, protect and guide us.*

[Celebrant] God of strength and courage hear our prayers through the intercession of St George through Christ our Lord.

R/. *Amen.*

■ LITURGY OF THE EUCHARIST

Preparation of the Altar and procession with the Gifts *Music*

Prayer over the Gifts

Father, receive these gifts we offer on the feast of St George and make them and us pleasing to you.
We ask this through Christ our Lord.

R/. *Amen.*

Eucharistic Prayer
Eucharistic Prayer for Children I

We give thanks for the ministry of Jesus and allow him to touch our lives.

Prayer after Communion

Lord, in this Eucharist we touch the divine life you offer us. Strengthen us to proclaim your love and peace.
We ask this through Christ our Lord.

R/. *Amen.*

■ CONCLUDING RITES

Blessing

Dismissal

Recessional hymn

"Leader now on earth no longer"

[Celebration Hymnal for Everyone, no.352]

2 TEACHER'S NOTES

Background

SAINT GEORGE, a fourth century martyr, was much venerated in the Christian East. Pictures of St George, usually show him overcoming a great dragon, a legendary figure which has always symbolised evil.

In Islam George is given the honoured title "prophet." He has been known in England at least from the eighth century.

Crusaders discovered devotion to George and brought it back to England. He has been patron of England at least from the reign of Edward III (1327-1377). The George chapel in Windsor dates from 1347.

Central focus

George recalls the unending battle with the powers of evil. It is in the Mass that we take up the weapons of Christ and are to be clothed with the armour of God (see Eph. 6:10-19).

Readings

The reading from Romans speaks about the battle against evil in which like George, we must be involved. Serving the Lord and abiding in love we will conquer evil with good. The main Christian weapon is the Cross which redeems us, and which we too must carry.

Offertory

Procession with symbols and gifts:
- ❍ St George Cross (red cross against a while background).
- ❍ Map of England.
- ❍ English symbols, e.g. of Royalty, Parliament, sport, culture.
- ❍ List of pupils and staff with the name George.
- ❍ English rose.
- ❍ Bread and wine.

Eucharistic Prayer
Eucharistic Prayer for Children I

We give thanks for the ministry of Jesus and allow him to touch our lives.

Sanctus Acclamation	*Sung*
Memorial Acclamation	*Sung*
Great Amen	*Sung*
Communion	*Music*

Follow up

To be aware of my need of protection from evil; invoke St George or Guardian Angel.

3 CELEBRANT'S NOTES

Background

INTRODUCTION TO MASS

ONCE A YEAR we hear questions about why St George is patron of England. The connections seem tenuous. But he is also patron saint of Venice, Genoa, Portugal, Catalonia and he is very much venerated in Russia and Ethiopia. There is not much hard historical evidence about events in his life. But he is immensely important as a symbol for the Christian life: conquering a dragon, the representation of evil, is the task of every saint, and of every Christian. From about the eight century there was devotion in England, increasing in the 14th century when we have the George Chapel at Windsor, the George Cross, the Order of the Garter (with St George as patron) and the battle cry of Edward III, 'St George for England.' Pope Benedict XII (1740-1758) proclaimed him Patron of England.

Readings

The readings take up the central symbolism of the life of George, his battle and victory against evil. The Gospel shows us the weapon of the Christian: it is the Cross which conquers evil and it is taking up the Cross and following Jesus that ensures our victory.

Homily pointers

The homily could take up the theme of the battle against evil:
○ The British armed services are for the defence of the country and to act as peacekeepers elsewhere in the world, especially under the United Nations flag.
○ There is a much more dangerous war than that of guns: the powers of evil seek to destroy our society from within through greed, drugs, violence, selfishness, racial divisions...
○ The Christian needs to take up the armour which God supplies to fight against wicked spiritual forces: stand ready... with truth as a belt tight round your waist... righteousness as breastplate... shod with the readiness to announce the good news of peace... faith as a shield to extinguish the burning arrows of the Evil One... helmet of salvation... as sword the word of God... prayer on every occasion" (see Ephesians 6:10-18).
○ Love of country and respect for other citizens is a Christian duty.

Communion reflection

Ask Jesus to make you strong against evil and upright in society.

Dismissal

If I see a George flag or a Union flag, say a prayer for my country of origin or adoption.

SS. PETER AND PAUL

1 LITURGY

Opening hymn

Follow me, follow me,
Leave your home and family,
Leave your fishing nets and boats
upon the shore.
Leave the seed that you have sown,
Leave the crops that you've grown,
Leave the people you have known
and follow me.

[Celebration Hymnal for Everyone no.175]

■ INTRODUCTORY RITES

Greeting

Penitential Rite

Lord Jesus, you assure us always of your
mercy.
R/. Lord have mercy.

Lord Jesus, you free us from all selfishness.
R/. Christ have mercy.

Lord Jesus, you call us to follow you closely.
R/. Lord have mercy.

Gloria

Opening prayer

God of compassion we celebrate the feast of
Peter and Paul. They left all to follow Jesus and
lived and died preaching the Gospel message.
Through their prayers help us to be courageous
in following you.
We ask this through Jesus Christ our Lord, who
lives and reigns with you and the Holy Spirit,
one God, for ever and ever.
R/. Amen.

■ LITURGY OF THE WORD

First Reading
Acts 12:1-11

About this time King Herod began to persecute
some members of the church. He had James,
the brother of John, put to death by the sword.
When he saw that this pleased the Jews, he
went on to arrest Peter. (This happened during
the time of the Festival of Unleavened Bread.)
After his arrest Peter was put in jail, where he
was handed over to be guarded by four groups
of four soldiers each. Herod planned to put him
on trial in public after Passover. So Peter was
kept in jail, but the people of the church were
praying earnestly to God for him. The night
before Herod was going to bring him out to the
people, Peter was sleeping between two guards.
He was tied with two chains, and there were
guards on duty at the prison gate. Suddenly an
angel of the Lord stood there, and a light shone
in the cell. The angel shook Peter by the
shoulder, woke him up, and said, "Hurry! Get
up!" At once the chains fell off Peter's hands.
Then the angel said, "Fasten your belt and put
on your sandals." Peter did so, and the angel
said, "Put your cloak round you and come with
me." Peter followed him out of the prison, not
knowing, however, if what the angel was doing
was real; he thought he was seeing a vision.
They passed by the first guard-post and then
the second, and came at last to the iron gate
leading into the city. The gate opened for them
by itself, and they went out. They walked down
a street, and suddenly the angel left Peter.

This is the Word of the Lord.
R/. Thanks be to God.

Responsorial Psalm
Psalm 116

R/. You Lord will rescue me.

Give thanks to the Lord with harps.
Sing to him with stringed instruments.
Sing a new song to him,
Play the harp with skill, and shout for joy!
R/. You Lord will rescue me.

The works of the Lord are true and all
His works are dependable.
The Lord loves what is righteous and just;
His constant love fills the earth.

> *R/. You Lord will rescue me.*

Second Reading   *2 Timothy 4:6-8, 17-18*

As for me, the hour has come for me to be sacrificed; the time is here for me to leave this life. I have done my best in the race, I have run the full distance, and I have kept the faith. And now there is waiting for me the victory prize of being put right with God, which the Lord, the righteous Judge, will give me on that Day – and not only to me, but to all those who wait with love for him to appear. The Lord stayed with me and gave me strength, so that I was able to proclaim the full message for all the Gentiles to hear; and I was rescued from being sentenced to death. And the Lord will rescue me from all evil and take me safely into his heavenly Kingdom. To him be the glory for ever and ever! Amen.

This is the Word of the Lord.

> *R/. Thanks be to God.*

Gospel Acclamation   *Sung*

Alleluia, Alleluia!
You are Peter and on this rock I will build my Church. And the gates of the underworld can never hold out against it.
Alleluia!

Gospel   *Matthew 16:13-19*

Jesus went to the territory near the town of Caesarea Philippi, where he asked his disciples, "Who do people say the Son of Man is?" "Some say John the Baptist," they answered. "Others say Elijah, while others say Jeremiah or some other prophet." "What about you?" he asked them, "who do you say I am?" Simon Peter answered, "You are the Messiah, the Son of the living God." "Good for you, Simon son of John!" answered Jesus. "For this truth did not come to you from any human being, but it was given to you directly by my Father in heaven. And so, I tell you, Peter: you are a rock, and on this rock

foundation I will build my church, and not even death will be able to overcome it. I will give you the keys of the Kingdom of heaven; what you prohibit on earth will be prohibited in heaven, and what you permit on earth will be permitted in heaven."

This is the Gospel of the Lord.

> *R/. Praise to you, Lord Jesus Christ.*

Prayer of the Faithful

[Celebrant] Loving Father, we praise and thank you for the example of Ss Peter and Paul hear us as we pray:

> *R/. You have the message of eternal life.*

For our Pope and Bishop that their lives will be marked by loving service.

> *R/. You have the message of eternal life.*

For all who like St Paul work as missionaries.

> *R/. You have the message of eternal life.*

For all who feel unworthy followers of Jesus.

> *R/. You have the message of eternal life.*

For fishermen and tent-makers and for the people of Rome and Malta.

> *R/. You have the message of eternal life.*

For all who have died, that having fought the good fight to the end, they may receive the crown of glory.

> *R/. You have the message of eternal life.*

For ourselves, that we may be inspired by the witness of Peter and follow you closely.

> *R/. You have the message of eternal life.*

[Celebrant] Almighty God, you called and raised up Ss Peter and Paul to be our leaders in faith. Listen favourably to the prayers we make on their feast, through Christ our Lord.

> *R/. Amen.*

▪ LITURGY OF THE EUCHARIST

Preparation of the Altar and procession with the Gifts   *Music*

Prayer over the Gifts

Lord accept these gifts in memory of St Peter and St Paul. Make us truly holy by this Eucharist and lead us to eternal praise of you.
We ask this through Christ our Lord.

> *R/. Amen.*

Eucharistic Prayer

Eucharistic Prayer for Children I
with Preface of Ss Peter and Paul.

Prayer after Communion

Father you give us light through the noble teaching and example of Ss Peter and Paul. In this sacrament we have received awaken in us a zeal to preach your Gospel.
We ask this in the name of Jesus the Lord.

> *R/. Amen.*

▪ CONCLUDING RITES

Blessing

Dismissal

Recessional hymn

"Follow me, follow me"

[Celebration Hymnal for Everyone no.175]

2 TEACHER'S NOTES

Background

THE FOUNDATIONS of the Church of Rome were the apostles Peter and Paul. Peter was called the foundation, the Rock, by Jesus. Paul was the great missionary and the theologian who wrote the major letters of the New Testament. He was shipwrecked on Malta. Both were martyred in Rome in the 60s of the first century, Peter it is said by crucifixion, Paul by being beheaded.

Central focus

As the Church celebrates the Mass, it recalls its foundation in these two apostles.

Readings

The readings help us to grasp the importance of the apostles in the early Church. The first from the Acts of the Apostles tells of the dramatic escape of Peter from prison through God's angel. The second is a reflection on his ministry set in Paul's last years. The Gospel is the establishment of the Church on Peter by Jesus.

Offertory

Procession with symbols and gifts:
- ○ Picture/model of boat and fishing net.
- ○ Keys.
- ○ Letters of St Paul in New Testament.
- ○ Picture of Pope.
- ○ Bread and wine.

Eucharistic Prayer

Eucharistic Prayer for Children I
with Preface of Sts Peter and Paul.

The Preface always tells us why today we give thanks at Mass.

Acclamation   *Sung*

Memorial Acclamation   *Sung*

Great Amen   *Sung*

Communion   *Music*

Follow up

We need to pray for the Pope and our bishop.

3 CELEBRANT'S NOTES

Background

INTRODUCTION TO THE MASS

WE DON'T often find statues or pictures of St Peter or St Paul in churches or classrooms. Popes invoke their prayers, but maybe not ordinary Catholics. But they are very important saints, indicated by their feast being a holiday of obligation in Britain and many other countries in Europe. They are fascinating figures and we can see them coming to life in the pages of the New Testament. Both had shaky beginnings: Peter denied Jesus; Paul persecuted the Church. But in God's plan they were to be the foundation of the Church.

Readings

The readings are vivid and dramatic.
The reading from Acts is an account of Peter's escape from jail with the help of an angel sent by God. The second reading presents us with Paul's reflection as an old man looking back on God's grace to him personally and for his mission. The Gospel, which tells us how Jesus was going to build his Church on Peter, opens with a hard question for the apostles and for us, *"Who do you say that I am?"*

Homily pointers

One could look at the careers of Peter and Paul and draw reflections for our time:

○ They are the foundation of the Church; we should read their writings.

○ They founded the Church of Rome; we need to pray for our Pope and bishop.

○ Both sinned and were forgiven and given responsible tasks for the Church; forgiven sinners are often God's best servants.

○ God protected their mission, even though he did not make it easy for them; we need to trust in difficulties.

○ Peter was a fisherman; Paul a tent-maker and a writer; we all have gifts to be used for others.

○ Peter was challenged by Jesus' question, "Who do you say I am?" Who is Jesus for me? Lord, judge, friend, distant acquaintance… ? (Cardinal Hume asked: "Is Jesus a weekday friend or a Sunday acquaintance?").

○ Peter and Paul died for the Church; do we love the Church?

Communion reflection

Ask Jesus to give us a deep love for his Church.

Dismissal

When we see something about the Church on the TV or newspapers, whisper a prayer, "Bless the Church, Lord."

ST. ANDREW

1 LITURGY

Opening hymn

Great Saint Andrew, friend of Jesus,
Lover of his glorious cross,
Early by his voice effective,
Called from ease to pain and loss.
Strong St Andrew, Simon's brother,
Who with haste fraternal flew,
Fain with him to share the treasure,
Which, at Jesus' lips he drew.

Loved St Andrew, Scotland's patron,
Watch thy land with heedful eye,
Rally round the cross of Jesus
All her storied chivalry!
To the Father, Son and Spirit,
Fount of sanctity and love,
Give we glory, now and ever,
With the saints who reign above.

[Celebration Hymnal for Everyone, no.232]

■ INTRODUCTORY RITES

Greeting

Penitential Rite

You call us to leave selfishness and sin.
  R/. Lord have mercy.

You invite us to follow you closely
  R/. Christ have mercy.

You offer us forgiveness and compassion.
  R/. Lord have mercy.

Opening prayer

Creator God, your Son Jesus called Andrew
the apostle to preach the good news.
May his prayers in your presence give us
courage to follow you.
We ask this through Jesus Christ our Lord
who lives and reigns with you in the unity of
the Holy Spirit one God for ever and ever.
  R/. Amen.

■ LITURGY OF THE WORD

First Reading   *Romans 10:9.14-15*

If you confess that Jesus is Lord and believe that
God raised him from death, you will be saved,
But how can they call to him for help if they
have not believed? And how can they believe if
they have not heard the message? And how can
they hear if the message is not proclaimed? And
how can the message be proclaimed if the
messengers are not sent out? As the scripture
says, "How wonderful is the coming of
messengers who bring good news."

This is the Word of the Lord.
  R/. Thanks be to God.

Responsorial Psalm   *Psalm 18*

  R/. Reverence the Lord at all times.

How clearly the sky reveals God's glory,
How plainly it shows what he has done.
  R/. Reverence the Lord at all times.

No speech or words are used,
no sound is heard;
Yet their message goes out to all the world.
  R/. Reverence the Lord at all times.

Reverence for the Lord is good.
It will continue forever.
The judgements of the Lord are just;
They are always fair.
  R/. Reverence the Lord at all times.

Gospel Acclamation *Sung*

Alleluia! Alleluia!
Follow me and I will teach you to catch
people for love of me.
Alleluia!

Gospel *Matthew 4:18-22*

As Jesus walked along the shore of Lake Galilee, he saw two brothers who were fishermen, Simon (called Peter) and his brother Andrew, catching fish in the lake with a net. Jesus said to them, "Come with me and I will teach you to catch people." At once they left their nets and went with him. He went on and saw two other brothers, James and John, the sons of Zebedee. They were in their boat with their father, Zebedee, getting their nets ready. Jesus called them, and at once they left the boat and their father, and went with him.

This is the Gospel of the Lord.

R/. Praise to you, Lord Jesus Christ.

Prayer of the Faithful

[Celebrant] God of love you search for us as we pray:

That the Church in Scotland may proclaim your love.

R/. You search for us and call us by name.

That political leaders may follow your values.

R/. You search for us and call us by name.

That the people of Scotland may cherish their culture.

R/. You search for us and call us by name.

That fishermen and all who work at sea may be safe.

R/. You search for us and call us by name.

That the Royal National Lifeboat Institution may continue its great work for those in danger at sea.

R/. You search for us and call us by name.

That we will treasure our faith and follow the inspiration of St Andrew.

R/. You search for us and call us by name.

[Celebrant] Loving Father hear our prayers which we make through Christ our Lord.

R/. Amen.

▦ LITURGY OF THE EUCHARIST

Preparation of the Altar and procession with the gifts *Music*

Prayer over the Gifts

Father, receive these gifts we offer on the feast of St Andrew and make them and us pleasing to you.
We ask this through Christ our Lord.

R/. Amen.

Eucharistic Prayer

Eucharistic Prayer for Children I
with Preface of the Apostles.

We give thanks for the ministry of the apostles.

Prayer after Communion

Lord, we thank you for this sacrament of love. May we be courageous in our following of you now and always.
We ask this in the name of Jesus the Lord.

R/. Amen.

■ CONCLUDING RITES

Blessing

Dismissal

Recessional hymn

"Follow me, follow me."

[Celebration Hymnal for Everyone no.175]

2 TEACHER'S NOTES

Background

ST ANDREW and his brother St Peter were Galilean fishermen who were given a new commission by Jesus: they were now to fish for people. Among the Twelve apostles, Peter and Andrew were especially close to Jesus. Andrew devoted himself to missionary work after Pentecost in various countries.

It is said that he died on an X-shaped cross, which is still retained in the national flag of Scotland. He is one of the patrons of Russia, which he never visited; it is unlikely that he visited Scotland either. A legend tells that his relics were brought to Scotland; the place was later called St Andrews.

Central focus

The call to discipleship given to Andrew is also given to all of us, and nourished in the Eucharist.

Readings

The first reading from St Paul's letter to the Romans outlines the need for, and the beauty of, preaching the good news. The Gospel tells the story of the calling of Andrew to be a different kind of fisherman.

Offertory

Procession with symbols and gifts.
- ○ Symbols of Scotland e.g. Andrew Cross, tartan.
- ○ Symbols of fishing.
- ○ Map of Scotland.
- ○ Photograph of Scottish Assembly.
- ○ List of pupils and staff with the name "Andrew."
- ○ Banner with Jesus' invitation "Come follow me."

Eucharistic Prayer
Eucharistic Prayer for Children I
with Preface of the Apostles.

We give thanks for the ministry of the apostles.

Sanctus Acclamation	*Sung*
Memorial Acclamation	*Sung*
Great Amen	*Sung*
Communion	*Sung*

Follow up

How am I to be a good Christian and a good citizen?

3 CELEBRANT'S NOTES

Background

INTRODUCTION TO THE MASS

NATIONAL feast days are a time of celebration and reflection on our calling and duties as Christians and as citizens. It cannot be established that St Andrew has direct links with Scotland, though there is a legend that his relics were brought to St Andrews. There is a strong and credible tradition about his missionary work around the Eastern Mediterranean and Middle East. Tradition also speaks of his martyrdom on an X-shaped cross.

Readings

The first reading is Paul's celebration that the good news has been preached.
Every generation needs the triple activity of preaching, hearing and believing.
The Gospel tells of the call of Andrew.

Homily pointers

One could speak about citizenship and Christian commitment:
- Pride of nationality and culture.
- Civic duty as a Christian duty.

One might also point up the various references to Andrew in the Gospel:
- A disciple of John the Baptist.
- He told Simon that he had found the Messiah and took him to Jesus (John 1:35-42).
- He is called to change the direction of his work: from Galilee fishing to making catches for the Kingdom (Matt. 4:18-22).
- He is part of an inner group of apostles especially close to Jesus: Peter, James, John, Andrew.
- He brings Philip's observations to Jesus (John 12:20-22)

Communion reflection

Ask Jesus how I am to follow him; ask him for the strength to do so.

Dismissal

Pride in nationality, pride in being a follower of Jesus.

2 | OCCASIONS

OPENING OF SCHOOL YEAR

1 LITURGY

Opening hymn

On this school your blessing, Lord;
on this school your grace bestow.
On this school your blessing, Lord;
may it come and never go.
Bringing peace and joy and happiness,
bringing love that knows no end.
On this school your blessing, Lord;
on this school your blessing send.

*[Celebration Hymnal for Everyone no.567
with "house" changed to school]*

© 1979 Joseph Weinberger Ltd.

■ INTRODUCTORY RITES

Greeting

Penitential Rite

Lord God, at the beginning you created men
and women to be like you.

R/. Lord have mercy.

Lord God, all people have sinned and turned
from your way.

R/. Christ have mercy.

Lord God, you continually offer us new
beginnings.

R/. Lord have mercy.

Opening prayer

Creator God, source of all light and
inspiration, lead and guide us through this
new school year. Help us to know your will
and follow it with courage.
We ask this through our Lord Jesus Christ
your Son who lives and reigns with you and
the Holy Spirit, one God for ever and ever.

R/. Amen.

■ LITURGY OF THE WORD

First Reading   *Acts 7:20-22*

Moses was cared for at home for three months,
and when he was put out of his home, the king's
daughter adopted him and brought him up as
her own son. He was taught all the wisdom of
the Egyptians and became a great man in words
and deeds.

This is the Word of the Lord.

R/. Thanks be to God.

Responsorial Psalm   *Psalm 37:23-24.30*

R/. Lord teach me your ways.

The Lord guides us in the way we should go,
And protects those who please him.

R/. Lord teach me your ways.

If they fall they will not stay down
Because the Lord will help them up.

R/. Lord teach me your ways.

Good people's words are wise
And are always fair.
They keep the law of God in their heart
And never depart from it.

R/. Lord teach me your ways.

Gospel Acclamation   *Sung*

Alleluia, Alleluia, Alleluia!
Lord, teach us your ways,
 you have the message of eternal life.
Alleluia.

Gospel   *Matthew 13:54-55*

Jesus taught in the synagogue, and those who heard him were amazed. "Where did he get such wisdom?" they asked. "And what about his miracles? Isn't he the carpenter's son? Isn't Mary his mother?"

This is the Gospel of the Lord.

R/. Praise to you Lord Jesus Christ.

Prayer of the Faithful

[Celebrant] Gracious God, our great protector, hear us as we pray:

R/. Lord let your face shine on us.

That our work and play will be blessed this year.

R/. Lord let your face shine on us.

That our school community will reflect Gospel values.

R/. Lord let your face shine on us.

That all new pupils and staff will feel welcome and supported.

R/. Lord let your face shine on us.

That we will be open to your Holy Spirit in our study and learning.

R/. Lord let your face shine on us.

That through the intercession of Mary we may be faithful followers of Jesus.

R/. Lord let your face shine on us.

[Celebrant] Loving God listen to our prayers and let your face shine on us through Christ our Lord.

R/. Amen.

◼ LITURGY OF THE EUCHARIST

Preparation of the Altar and procession of Gifts   *Music*

Prayer over Gifts

Father, accept these gifts as we begin a new school year. Help us to recognise Christ in this Eucharist and welcome him with love. We ask this through Christ our Lord.

R/. Amen.

Eucharistic Prayer

Children's Masses III – Outside Easter

Prayer after Communion

Father, in this Eucharist you touch our lives. Keep your love alive in our hearts as we begin this school year.
We ask this in the name of your Son our Lord.

R/. Amen.

◼ CONCLUDING RITES

Blessing

Dismissal

Recessional hymn

'How lovely on the mountains.'

[Celebration Hymnal for Everyone no.268]

② TEACHER'S NOTES

Background

A BEGINNING can be exciting, but it can also be a source of anxiety: how will it go? The year ahead will certainly be different from what we expect.

Even experienced teachers can never predict how a year will unfold. Teachers might ask the pupils what are their hopes, fears and dreams for the coming year. At this beginning of the year we look to God's help and we prepare to adapt ourselves to whatever comes about.

Central focus

The Eucharist is the meeting place between God and ourselves. Each Mass is a new beginning.

Readings

The scripture readings are about two remarkable children and their education: Moses and Jesus. Moses was taught by the Pharaoh's daughter. Jesus was taught by Joseph and Mary. Both depended on their teachers and grew in wisdom.

Offertory

Procession with symbols and gifts:
- ○ Mission statement.
- ○ A new writing book with pen and pencil.
- ○ School tie or scarf or crest.
- ○ Bread and wine to be changed into the Body and Blood of the Lord.

Eucharistic Prayer

The Christian gives thanks (Eucharist) for all the good gifts of creation, and especially for Jesus who saved us and stays with us.
He is with us now as we begin the year.

Sanctus Acclamation	*Sung*
Memorial Acclamation	*Sung*
Great Amen	*Sung*
Communion	*Music*

Follow up

Display and focus on School Mission Statement in class.
Ongoing reference to theme of Mass and homily in the days ahead.

3 CELEBRANT'S NOTES

Background

INTRODUCTION TO MASS

BEGINNING the school year with Mass is an indication of the place of the Eucharist in our lives. The Church teaches that it is "the source and the culmination of the whole Christian life." (Vatican II, *Church* LG 11). We are bringing our hopes, dreams and fears; we offer ourselves and the year to God. From this Mass we expect to focus ourselves and to get strength for the year ahead.

Readings

In the first reading we see the young Moses. His life was in danger and he was adopted by a stranger who cared for him. He became great in word and deed, eventually liberating his people.

The Gospel reading tells of the wonder of the villagers at Nazareth at the wisdom and power of Jesus. They thought little of Joseph and Mary: their Son could not be significant!

Homily pointers

The God of surprises:
- ❍ Pharaoh's daughter did not know how the boy she saved would turn out. She was a good foster mother to him.
- ❍ The village people at Nazareth did not have any idea that the boy they knew playing around was going to be the great figure of the Messiah.
- ❍ Parents do not know either how their children will turn out.
- ❍ Teachers and school can only do a limited amount for pupils. In the end it will depend on you, on the choices you make, how your life will turn out.

- ❍ Whatever the future holds, during the coming year or throughout our lives, we will find strength and wisdom by attending Mass attentively.
- ❍ A good rule when we are thinking of doing something is to say, "can I offer this thing to Jesus at Mass? Will he be pleased with it?"

Communion reflection

Jesus I offer you the year ahead.
I know that you will walk with me.
Teach me your ways.
Help me to continue to look to you
for light and guidance.

Dismissal

A parting thought: Jesus is with us. We can always find him in Church and in our hearts.

[Thanks to those who prepared the liturgy and participated in it.]

HARVEST TIME

1 LITURGY

Opening hymn

In the earth the small seed is hidden and
Lies unseen until it is bidden by
Springtime stirrings up to the sunlight and
Summer ripening.
Golden is the harvest and precious the
Bread that you are and give to us, Lord.

[Celebration Hymnal for Everyone no.306]

© *McCrimmon Publishing Co., Ltd.*

■ INTRODUCTORY RITES

Greeting

Penitential Rite

Lord Jesus, you created the world and all its
    creatures.
   R/. Lord have mercy.

Lord Jesus, you made us in your own image
    and likeness.
   R/. Christ have mercy.

Lord Jesus, you open our eyes to the beauty of
    your handiwork.
   R/. Lord have mercy.

Opening prayer

God of the heavens and earth we thank you
for the richness of harvest time and for food.
May the fruitfulness of this time make us
thankful for your constant love and care for
us.
We ask this through our Lord Jesus Christ,
your Son, who lives and reigns with you and
the Holy Spirit, one God, for ever and ever.
   R/. Amen.

■ LITURGY OF THE WORD

First Reading
James 3:17-18

The wisdom from above is pure first of all; it is
also peaceful, gentle, and friendly; it is full of
compassion and produces a harvest of good
deeds. And goodness is the harvest that is
produced from the seeds the peacemakers plant
in peace.

This is the Word of the Lord.
   R/. Thanks be to God.

Responsorial Psalm
Psalm 67

   R/. May the peoples praise you, O God.

God be merciful and bless us;
Look on us with kindness,
So that the whole world may know your will;
So that all nations may know your salvation.
   R/. May the peoples praise you, O God.

The land has produced its harvest
God, our God, has blessed us.
God has blessed us;
May the people everywhere honour him.
   R/. May the peoples praise you, O God.

Gospel Acclamation
Sung
Alleluia, Alleluia!

The earth has yielded its fruit,
God our God has blessed us.
Alleluia.

Gospel
Matthew 9:37

Jesus said to his disciples, "The harvest is large,
but there are few workers to gather it in. Pray to
the owner of the harvest that he will send out
workers to gather in his harvest."

This is the Gospel of the Lord.
   R/. Praise to you, Lord Jesus Christ.

Prayer of the Faithful

[Celebrant] Divine Giver of fruitfulness, you bless the earth and provide for our needs hear our prayer.

R/. Lord of the harvest, we thank you.

That we may receive the gifts of the earth with thankfulness.

R/. Lord of the harvest, we thank you.

That the earth's produce will be generously shared.

R/. Lord of the harvest, we thank you.

That all who work on the land will be treated justly.

R/. Lord of the harvest, we thank you.

That we will always respect the earth.

R/. Lord of the harvest, we thank you.

That we may be generous in helping the hungry and poor.

R/. Lord of the harvest, we thank you.

[Celebrant] Creator of all that is good, listen favourably to our prayers we make through Christ our Lord.

R/. Amen.

▪ LITURGY OF THE EUCHARIST

Preparation of the Altar and procession of Gifts
Music

Prayer over Gifts

Lord, make holy the gifts we offer with gratitude from the fruitfulness of the earth. As you have made our land bear a rich harvest, make our hearts fruitful with your life and love.
We ask this in the name of Jesus, the Lord.

R/. Amen.

Eucharistic Prayer Children I

Prayer after Communion

Lord, we thank you for the fruits of the earth. May the power of this saving mystery bring us even greater gifts.
We ask this in the name of Jesus, the Lord.

R/. Amen.

▪ CONCLUDING RITES

Blessing

Dismissal

Recessional hymn

'Glorious God King of creation.'

[Celebration Hymnal for Everyone no.194]

89

OCCASIONS

② TEACHER'S NOTES

Background

WE CANNOT take food for granted. Many people are without enough to live on. We all depend on farmers who till the soil, who care for animals which give us milk, food and nourishment. There was a time when the gathering of food was in the autumn, harvest time. Now there is sowing and gathering all-year-round. But there is still a time in autumn where there is more gathering than at other times. It is appropriate that we celebrate this time of blessing and give thanks. We should also remember those who are less well off than ourselves.

Central focus

The word "Eucharist" means thanksgiving. At this Mass we give thanks for fruit, vegetables, flowers, meat, farm produce, and the work of so many people – farmers, shops, delivery services.

Readings

The readings develop also a spiritual meaning of harvest. We are not just concerned with crops that feed us, but with the harvest of good works that all of us are called to produce. St James speaks of the harvest we should have if we are wise and follow God's way. The result of our efforts are to be peace.

The Gospel text shows Jesus looking at the harvest. Yes, we need labourers for the harvest and we pray for them. But there is also the spiritual harvest that is to be gained when people gather in with the word of God.

Offertory

Procession with symbols and gifts:
- ❍ A basket or hamper of food to be given later to some charitable organisation like St Vincent de Paul.
- ❍ One of various kinds of food (fresh, tinned, wrapped, dried).
- ❍ Fruit of the earth – bread and wine – to be transformed into the Body and Blood of the Lord.

Eucharistic Prayer

The preface gives reasons why today we give thanks. The Eucharistic Prayer for Children I celebrates the beauty of all creation, and goes on to remember all who are poor. All creation is enveloped with God's love and care.

Sanctus Acclamation	*Sung*
Memorial Acclamation	*Sung*
Great Amen	*Sung*
Communion	*Music*

Follow up

The pupils could be invited to write, sing or celebrate the wonder of creation. Greater attention could be given to news about starvation in various parts of the world.

3 CELEBRANT'S NOTES

Background

INTRODUCTION TO MASS

THERE will be quite a difference between rural and urban parishes. In country areas pupils will be very familiar with harvest times. In urban areas children may not know much about where food comes from, what is grown. The emphasis on the Mass is thanksgiving for food and remembrance of those who lack basics of life.

Readings

The harvest theme is expanded to include all fruitfulness. Not only is the earth to bring forth good things for us to eat. We are to be fruitful in good works.

Homily pointers

Grateful hearts:
- ○ Grace before meals: are we really grateful for each meal?
- ○ Look at the fruits and vegetables in your local shop: the beauty, the colour, the variety of God's gifts.
- ○ We depend on others so much: farmers produce food, lorries and trucks deliver them, shop keepers keep food fresh and wholesome, people cook for us.
- ○ We also benefit from people overseas especially for fruits that we cannot grow at home.
- ○ As we thank God for the food we have, we remember those who are struggling to survive.
- ○ Harvest is a symbol of our lives: we are to be fruitful in good works.

Communion reflection

Jesus you feed us with your own Body.
Give us strength in our minds and bodies.
Help us to be good to others.
Show us how to bear fruit in good works.

Dismissal

A parting thought: Look at food in a new way.

[Thanks to those who prepared the liturgy and participated in it.]

CHRISTIAN UNITY

1 LITURGY

Opening hymn

"Will you let me be your servant,"
let me be as Christ to you?
Pray that I may have the grace to
let you be my servant too.

We are pilgrims on a journey,
we are trav'llers on the road;
we are here to help each other
walk the mile and bear the load.

I will hold the Christ-light for you
in the night-time of your fear;
I will hold my hand out to you,
speak the peace you long to hear.

[Celebration Hymnal for Everyone no.813]

© 1977 Scripture in Song / Administered by Copycare.

■ INTRODUCTORY RITES

Greeting

Penitential Rite

You call us to love each other as you love us.

R/. Lord have mercy.

You have said that all who come to you will
never be turned away.

R/. Christ have mercy.

You taught us that there is one fold and one
Shepherd.

R/. Lord have mercy.

Opening prayer

Father of all, draw us closer to each other.
Strengthen the bonds that unite all peoples
and help us to seek you always as our loving
God.
We ask this through our Lord Jesus Christ
who lives and reigns with you and the Holy
Spirit, one God for ever and ever.

R/. Amen.

■ LITURGY OF THE WORD

First Reading   *Ephesians 4:3-6*

Do your best to preserve the unity which the
Spirit gives by means of the peace that binds
you together. There is one body and one Spirit,
Just as there is one hope to which God has
called you. There is one Lord, one faith, one
baptism; there is one God and Father of all.

This is the word of the Lord.

R/. Thanks be to God.

Responsorial Psalm   *Psalm 122:1-2*

R/. Let us go to God's House.

I was glad when they said to me,
"Let us go to the Lord's house."
And now we are here,
standing inside the gates of Jerusalem!

R/. Let us go to God's House.

Jerusalem is a city restored
in beautiful order and harmony.
This is where the tribes come,
the tribes of Israel,
to give thanks to the Lord.

R/. Let us go to God's House.

Pray for peace of Jerusalem;
"May those who love you prosper.
May there be peace inside your walls
and safety in your palaces."
For the sake of my relatives and friends
I say to Jerusalem, "Peace be with you!"

R/. Let us go to God's House.

Gospel Acclamation   *Sung*

Alleluia, Alleluia, Alleluia!
You are the people of God; he loved you
and chose you for his own.
Alleluia!

Gospel
John 17:21-23

At the Last Supper Jesus prayed, "I pray that they may all be one. Father! May they be in us, just as you are in me and I am in you. May they be one, so that the world may believe that you sent me. I gave them the glory you gave me, so that they may be one, just as you and I are one. I in them and you in me, so that they may be completely one, in order that the world may know that you sent me, and that you love them as you love me."

This is the Gospel of the Lord.

R/. Praise to you, Lord Jesus Christ.

Prayer of the Faithful

[Celebrant] Source of all unity and peace hear us as we pray:

R/. Help us to see and love you in our brothers and sisters.

That those who work for peace and unity in the Church will be supported.

R/. Help us to see and love you in our brothers and sisters.

That we will have the courage to listen openly to one another.

R/. Help us to see and love you in our brothers and sisters.

That we will be peacemakers and peace loving.

R/. Help us to see and love you in our brothers and sisters.

That Church leaders in this area will work for that unity for which Jesus prayed.

R/. Help us to see and love you in our brothers and sisters.

[Celebrant] Good and gracious Father hear our prayers and desires for greater unity and peace.
We ask this through Christ our Lord.

R/. Amen.

■ LITURGY OF THE EUCHARIST

Preparation of the altar and procession with the Gifts
Music

Prayer over the Gifts

Lord, renew in us the gifts of unity and peace. May we share your peace with others. We ask this through Christ, our Lord.

R/. Amen.

Eucharistic Prayer
Reconciliation II

Prayer after Communion

Lord, may this sacrament of love be our guide to peace and unity.
We ask this in the name of Jesus the Lord.

R/. Amen.

Blessing

Dismissal

Recessional hymn

Bind us together, Lord,   *(Chorus)*
bind us together with cords
that cannot be broken.
Bind us together, Lord,
bind us together,
bind us together with love.

There is only one God,
there is only one King,
there is only one Body,
that is why we sing:

Bind us...

[Celebration Hymnal for Everyone no.80]
© 1977 Thankyou Music / Administered by Worshiptogether.com songs

2 TEACHER'S NOTES

Background

THERE are many Christian Churches, but Jesus wanted all his followers to be one (see John 17). The disunity is a fact but there is a challenge to work for unity. Part of the work for unity is prayer; it also involves learning more about one another and respecting each other. The Christian Churches have Unity Week 18-25 January, as a time of special prayer. Prayer and interest in other Christians should not be confined to this time.

Central focus

We think of the Churches in our area:

- ❍ The Church of England is the Established Church in England: it has a long tradition for worship and love of the scripture.
- ❍ The Methodist Church is known for the prayer life of its members and for their social concern.
- ❍ The Orthodox Churches have a very ancient worship and praise God with splendid liturgy.
- ❍ The Baptist Churches have put great emphasis on faith.
- ❍ The Pentecostal Churches pay special attention to the gifts of the Holy Spirit.
- ❍ The Salvation Army is known for their great work for those in need.
- ❍ The Congregational Churches have a fine sense of involvement of members in the running of the Church.
- ❍ The Catholic Church is rich in doctrine and sacraments, and in the guidance it gets from pope and bishops.
- ❍ The Society of Friends (Quakers) are known for their prayer life and their passion for peace.

Would it not be great if we could all share the gifts of the different Churches! *(Groden – O'Donnell, School Assemblies vol.1, p80).* The Eucharist is where our divisions most clearly show; it is also to be the time when our prayer for unity should be most effective.

Offertory

Procession with symbols and gifts:

- ❍ Posters with names of Christian Churches in our locality.
- ❍ The bible common to all.
- ❍ A cross our common symbol.
- ❍ Bread from many grains, and wine from many grapes to become the one host and one cup.

Eucharist prayer

The Eucharist is word and sacrament.
We are quite united in word, but still divided in sacrament.

Holy, holy	*Sung*
Memorial Acclamation	*Sung*
Great Amen	*Sung*
Communion	*Music*

Follow up

In weeks ahead watch out for news and events in other Churches.

3 CELEBRANT'S NOTES

Background

INTRODUCTION TO MASS

THE ECUMENICAL movement was born in 1910 at Edinburgh when a group of Protestant mission-sending societies became acutely aware of divided witness. The Catholic Church did not become officially involved in the ecumenical movement until 1960 when Bl. John XXIII set up the Secretariat for Christian Unity. Vatican II taught the Church how to be ecumenical: Church renewal, love, prayer, conversion, dialogue, cooperation (See Vatican II, *Decree on Unity*, UR nn.5-11). Ecumenical action must not be confined to Unity Week, 18-25 January.

Readings

Two classical texts for unity are chosen. The letter to Ephesians gives the grounds for unity. John gives Jesus' prayer for unity.

Homily pointers

Ecumenism is:
- ○ Being interested in other Churches, sharing in joys and sorrows.
- ○ Caring about disunity
- ○ Working with other Christians.
- ○ Learning about and with other Christians.
- ○ Being agents for peace and reconciliation.
- ○ Sharing faith with other Christians.
- ○ Praying with other Christians.

Communion reflection

Jesus, we know that we should not be divided.
We do not know how to come together.
Show us the way of unity and peace.
Bless other Christians with your love.

Dismissal

A parting thought: As you pass a church or place of worship say: "Bless its congregation, Lord."

[Thanks to those who prepared the liturgy and participated in it.]

PEACE AND RECONCILIATION

1 LITURGY

Opening hymn

Peace, perfect peace, is the gift of Christ
our Lord *(x2)*
Thus says the Lord,
Will the world know my friends.
Peace, perfect peace,
Is the gift of Christ our Lord.

[Celebration Hymnal for Everyone no.597]

© Kevin Mayhew Ltd. Reproduced by permission from Hymns Old & New

■ INTRODUCTORY RITES

Greeting

Penitential Rite

Lord Jesus, you are Prince of Peace.

R/. Lord have mercy.

Lord Jesus, you are the way to peace and
reconciliation.

R/. Christ have mercy.

Lord Jesus, you are the rainbow of God's love
and forgiveness.

R/. Lord have mercy.

Opening prayer

God of peace and reconciliation, your light is
strong, your love is near. Heal the
brokenness in our lives.
We ask this through our Lord Jesus Christ,
your Son, who lives and reigns with you and
the Holy Spirit, one God, for ever and ever.

R/. Amen.

■ LITURGY OF THE WORD

First Reading
1 Thessalonians 5:22

May the God who gives us peace make you holy
in every way and keep your whole being, spirit,
soul, and body, free from every fault at the
coming of our Lord Jesus Christ. He who calls
you will do it, because he is faithful.

This is the Word of the Lord.

R/. Thanks be to God.

Responsorial Psalm

R/. Trust in the Lord and do good.

Trust in the Lord and do good;
live in the land and be safe.
Seek your happiness in the Lord,
and he will give you your heart's desire.

R/. Trust in the Lord and do good.

Give yourself to the Lord;
trust in him, and he will help you;
he will make your righteousness shine
like the noonday sun.

R/. Trust in the Lord and do good.

Soon the wicked will disappear;
you may look for them, but you won't find
them;
the humble will possess the land
and enjoy prosperity and peace.

R/. Trust in the Lord and do good.

Gospel Acclamation

Alleluia, Alleluia,   *Celtic (sung)*
Alleluia, Alleluia

Gospel
John 14:27

Jesus said: "Peace is what I leave with you; it is
my own peace that I give you. I do not give it as
the world does. Do not be worried or upset; do
not be afraid."

This is the Gospel of the Lord.

R/. Praise be to you, Lord Jesus Christ.

Prayer of the Faithful

[Celebrant] God of peace and healing hear our prayer:

For the Church that it may enjoy the gift of unity and peace.

R/. Make us instruments of your peace.

For peace in the world especially, the North of Ireland, the Holy Land and in *(name current places of unrest)*.

R/. Make us instruments of your peace.

For soldiers and police working with the United Nations, keeping peace in Africa.

R/. Make us instruments of your peace.

For neighbours who quarrel, for families who are divided and for people who find it hard to be at peace.

R/. Make us instruments of your peace.

For our homes and school that they will be havens of peace.

R/. Make us instruments of your peace.

For peace in our hearts.

R/. Make us instruments of your peace.

For all who have hurt us that we may be forgiving.

R/. Make us instruments of your peace.

[Celebrant] God of peace, you know that sin and weakness lead us into disorder and enmity; grant us the peace that your Son Jesus promised to his followers.
We ask this in his name.

R/. Amen.

■ LITURGY OF THE EUCHARIST

Preparation of the Altar and procession of Gifts
Music

Prayer over Gifts

Lord, accept our prayers and gifts.
Make us worthy of your peace and reconciliation.
We ask this through Christ our Lord.

R/. Amen.

Eucharistic Prayer and Preface
Eucharistic Prayer for Reconciliation II

The Preface tells us that today we should give thanks for God at work in our world.

Prayer after Communion

Father, we give thanks for the bread of life. Strengthen us to go out and serve you in peace and reconciliation.
We ask this in the name of Jesus the Lord.

R/. Amen.

■ CONCLUDING RITES

Blessing

Dismissal

Recessional hymn

'Lay your hands gently upon us.'

[Celebration Hymnal for Everyone no.347]

or

'Make me a channel of your peace.'

[Celebration Hymnal for Everyone no.478]

OCCASIONS

2 TEACHER'S NOTES

Background

THERE are different meanings of peace: a classroom might be very quiet, but the pupils uneasy; a cemetery is peaceful, but there is no life, even the birds do not seem cheerful; guns may be silent between countries or within countries, but there remains enmity and hatred. Christians often add "reconciliation" to peace, because without forgiveness, mutual acceptance and respect there will not be peace. We seek peace between nations, between people, within ourselves, with God. Peace is a gift for which we must pray.

Central focus

Several times in every Mass we pray for peace, most notably before Communion: "Lord Jesus Christ, you said to your apostles: 'I leave you peace, my peace I give you.' Look not on our sins, but on the faith of your Church, and grant us the peace and unity of your kingdom." The Mass is God's covenant and peace agreement with his people.

Readings

The first reading, from the earliest book of the New Testament, first Thessalonians, (ca. AD50) shows that even then Christians were conscious of their need for peace; the Gospel tells us that it is Jesus that gives the true peace.

Offertory

Procession with symbols and gifts:
- ❍ Names of places where there is conflict and need of peace and reconciliation.
- ❍ Names of peacemakers in school or families with members in the on peace missions.
- ❍ Map or globe.
- ❍ Cardboard cut out of doves as symbols of peace.
- ❍ Cut-out with "Peace is…" "Reconciliation is…"
- ❍ Pictures: winding road, mountain or stepping stones, walls.
- ❍ Picture of harmony: playground, elderly people, sheep or fields.
- ❍ Bread and wine.

Eucharistic Prayer and Preface
Eucharistic Prayer for Reconciliation II

The Preface tells us that today we should give thanks for God at work in our world.

Sanctus Acclamation	*Sung*
Memorial Acclamation	*Sung*
Great Amen	*Sung*
Communion	*Music*

Follow up

To speak words of healing and peace when others are disturbed or angry.

3 CELEBRANT'S NOTES

Background

INTRODUCTION TO THE MASS

THIS congregation will have very different ideas of what peace might mean. They will be surrounded by anti-peace: violence, threats, anger, stories of war, violent videos, perhaps disruption at home. Again peace might seem dull, not "cool" but boring. The message of Jesus about peace needs to be stated: it is not something negative but positive harmony within ourselves, with others and with God. It is above all a gift of God. The way to peace will often mean admitting wrong and will involve forgiveness.

Readings

The Gospel tells us that peace is not something that will be in our power. It is a gift that Jesus offers to us. Even in the earliest book of the New Testament, Paul writes to the Thessalonians about walking in holiness and peace.

Homily pointers

The homily might show different ways of peace and point out various understandings pointing out the Christian way:

- ○ Peace as harmony: between people, with God, within ourselves.
- ○ Peace is not to be presumed but prayed for and worked at.
- ○ Peace to be practised: small acts of love and kindness may help towards reconciliation and peace.
- ○ It takes only one to pick a fight, but it takes two to have a fight; we need two for reconciliation.
- ○ Forgiveness, respect, justice, compassion, love and prayer are the foundation stones of peace.

Communion reflection

Ask Jesus to help me to be a peacemaker, leaving every situation the better for my presence.

Dismissal

Ponder the final words of the priest at Mass. Having heard the word of God, celebrated the Eucharist of Jesus, we are told: "Go in peace to love and serve the Lord."

[Thanks to those who prepared the liturgy and participated in it.]

OCCASIONS

FIRST COMMUNION TIME

1 LITURGY

Opening hymn

Bind us together, Lord,
bind us together with cords
that cannot be broken.
Bind us together, Lord,
bind us together,
bind us together with love.

There is only one God,
there is only one King,
there is only one Body.
that is why we sing:

Made for the glory of God,
purchased by his precious Son,
born with the right to be clean,
for Jesus the victory has won.

You are the family of God,
you are the promise divine,
you are God's chosen desire,
you are the glorious new wine.

[Celebration Hymnal for Everyone no.80]

© 1977 Thankyou Music / Administered by worshiptogether.com songs

■ INTRODUCTORY RITES

Greeting

Penitential Rite

You call us friends.
  R/. Lord have mercy.
You share your life with us.
  R/. Christ have mercy.
You invite us to walk closely with you.
  R/. Lord have mercy.

Opening prayer

Father, we come to celebrate the great gift
which your Son has left to his Church.
Help us to come to his sacrament with great
love on this special day and keep us close to
you always.
We ask this through Christ our Lord.
  R/. Amen.

First Reading   1 Corinthians 11:23-27

I received from the Lord the teaching that I
passed on to you: that the Lord Jesus, on the
night he was betrayed, took a piece of bread,
gave thanks to God, broke it, and said, "This is
my body, which is for you. Do this in memory of
me." In the same way, after supper he took the
cup and said, "This cup is God's new covenant,
sealed with my blood. Whenever you drink it, do
so in memory of me." This means that every
time you eat this bread and drink from this cup
you proclaim the Lord's death until he comes.

This is the Word of the Lord.
  R/. Thanks be to God.

Responsorial Psalm   Psalm 117:1-2

  R/. Praise the Lord all you nations.

Praise the Lord, all nations!
Praise him, all peoples!
  R/. Praise the Lord all you nations.

His love for us is strong
and his faithfulness is eternal.
  R/. Praise the Lord all you nations.

Gospel Acclamation   Sung

Alleluia, Alleluia, Alleluia!
I am the Bread of Life, all who come to me
will never be turned away.
Alleluia!

100

Gospel

John 6:51-52

Jesus said, "I am the living bread that came down from heaven. Whoever eats this bread, will live for ever. The bread that I will give is my flesh, which I give so that the world may live."

This is the Gospel of the Lord.

R/. Praise to you Lord Jesus Christ.

Prayer of the Faithful

[Celebrant] We turn to our Risen Lord and pray.

R/. For you are the Bread of Life.

We pray for our bishop and priests.

R/. For you are the Bread of Life.

We pray for all who help out in our parish.

R/. For you are the Bread of Life.

We pray for all who have turned away from you.

R/. For you are the Bread of Life.

We pray for all who have prepared us for this day.

R/. For you are the Bread of Life.

We pray for all who have been good to us.

R/. For you are the Bread of Life.

[Celebrant] Father of us all hear these prayers which we make through Jesus the Bread of Life.

R/. Amen.

◼ LITURGY OF THE EUCHARIST

Preparation of the Altar and procession with the gifts

Music

Prayer over the Gifts

Lord, accept these gifts we offer.
May they draw us closer to you today and always.
We ask this through Christ our Lord. Amen.

R/. Amen.

Eucharistic Prayer and Preface

Preface of the Holy Eucharist I or II
Children's Masses III
"Outside the Easter Season".

Prayer after Communion

Lord, we thank you for coming to us in Holy Communion. May we always recognise Jesus in the Eucharist and welcome him with love for he is Lord forever and ever.

R/. Amen.

◼ CONCLUDING RITES

Blessing

Dismissal

Recessional hymn

My God loves me.
His love will never end.
He rests within my heart
for my God loves me.

His gentle hand
he stretches over me.
Though storm-clouds threaten the day
he will set me free.

He comes to me
in sharing bread and wine.
He brings me life that will reach
past the end of time.

My God loves me,
his faithful love endures.
And I will live like a child
held in love secure.

The joys of love
as offerings now we bring.
The pains of love will be lost
in the praise we sing.

[Celebration Hymnal for Everyone no.499]
v2-5 © 1978 Kevin Mayhew Ltd. Reproduced by permission from Hymns Old & New

OCCASIONS

② TEACHER'S NOTES

Background

FIRST COMMUNION is a great day in the life of a Christian. There is so much preparation so that the pupil will know what the day means, who Jesus is, and how he is to be welcomed and loved. Gifts and clothes are very secondary. We can reinforce the religious meaning of the day by emphasising the celebration and the event. This Mass is for those who are preparing/have received their First Communion. But it involves the rest of the school/parish who can look forward to their big day, or remember their own First Communion. An emphasis on the scripture will help to counteract excessive secular dimensions of the day.

Central focus

The whole Mass in which we are taught by the scriptures and in the homily, so that we can offer Jesus' sacrifice and meet him in Holy Communion.

Readings

The first reading is a catechism lesson that St Paul learned and passed on in turn to the Corinthian Church: it is an account of the Last Supper at which Christ gave us the gift of Holy Communion. The Gospel tells us that receiving Holy Communion will bring us to heaven.

Offertory

Procession with symbols and gifts, such as:

- ○ Symbols of Eucharistic programme: work book, posters.
- ○ Basket of flowers.
- ○ Key of Tabernacle on tray covered with white cloth.
- ○ Names of teachers/catechists who have prepared the Holy Communion candidates.
- ○ Bread and wine.

Eucharistic Prayer

Preface of the Holy Eucharist I or II
Children's Masses III
"Outside the Easter Season."

The Preface always tells us why today we give thanks at Mass.

Acclamation	*Sung*
Memorial Acclamation	*Sung*
Great Amen	*Sung*
Communion	*Music*

Follow up

Thanksgiving for Communion should continue during the day after Mass.
We ask Jesus to stay with us through his Holy Spirit.

3 CELEBRANT'S NOTES

Background

INTRODUCTION TO THE MASS

THE CELEBRANT may well feel negatively towards the expense and flamboyance of the First Communion event. But it is important to respect cultures and the need parents may feel of marking out a great day. An emphasis on the spiritual meaning of the day will therefore be important. It would be good to situate Holy Communion in the journey of initiation: Baptism, Confirmation and Eucharist and to show how the sacrament is to be integrated into the whole of the children's lives. The Mass will be attended by parents and teachers/catechists, who could be reminded of their own First Communion and about the role of the Eucharist in their lives.

Readings

The two readings give us the catechetical formula in the early Church which was given to Paul who in turn passed on; namely an account of the Last Supper. The Gospel has Jesus speaking of the gift which he will give to bring us to eternal life.

Homily pointers

The homily will focus on the First Communicants, but might also be evangelisation for parents.

- ○ Completion of Christian initiation.
- ○ Our spiritual food and drink.
- ○ Support for our journey of life.
- ○ Promise of eternal life.
- ○ Eucharist joins us with family members who have already passed to God.
- ○ Love of Communion and frequent reception.
- ○ Thanksgiving to continue from one Communion to another.

Communion reflection

Speak to Jesus. Welcome him into our hearts. Promise to love him.

Dismissal

After today, Jesus will be looking forward to the next time we receive Communion.

SCHOOL LEAVERS

1 LITURGY

Opening hymn

You are salt for the earth, O people;
salt for the Kingdom of God!
Share the flavour of life, O people;
life in the Kingdom of God.

Bring forth the Kingdom of mercy.
bring forth the Kingdom of peace;
bring forth the Kingdom of justice,
bring forth the City of God.

You are a light on the hill, O people:
light for the city of God!
Shine so holy and bright, O people:
shine for the Kingdom of God!

You are a seed of the Word, O people:
bring forth the Kingdom of God!
Seeds of mercy and seeds of justice,
grow in the Kingdom of God.

We are a blest and a pilgrim people;
Bound for the Kingdom of God!
Love our journey and love our homeland:
love is the Kingdom of God!

[Celebration Hymnal for Everyone no.821]

© 1986 GIA Publications Inc.

■ INTRODUCTORY RITES

Greeting

Penitential Rite

You showed us how to be loving.

R/. Lord have mercy.

You showed us how to be patient.

R/. Christ have mercy.

You showed us how to be generous.

R/. Lord have mercy.

Opening prayer

Father of love, protect us as we leave this school. Pour out your Spirit on us and guide us in your way of peace.
We ask this through our Lord Jesus Christ your Son who lives and reigns with you and the Holy Spirit one God for ever and ever.

R/. Amen.

First Reading   *Philippians 4:8-9*

Fill your minds with those things that are good and that deserve praise; things that are true, noble, right, pure, lovely and honourable. Put into practice what you learnt and received from me, both from my words and from my actions. And the God who gives us peace will be with you.

This is the word of the Lord.

R/. Thanks be to God.

Responsorial Psalm   *Psalm 46:1-5*

R/. God is our shelter and strength.

God is our shelter and strength,
always ready to help in times of trouble.
So we will not be afraid, even if the earth is
    shaken,
and mountains fall into the ocean depths;
even if the seas roar and rage,
and the hills are shaken by the violence.

R/. God is our shelter and strength.

There is a river that brings joy to the
    city of God,
to the sacred house of the Most High.
God is in that city, and it will never be
    destroyed;
at early dawn he will come to its aid.

R/. God is our shelter and strength.

Gospel Acclamation   *Sung*

"Celtic Alleluia"
or
Alleluia, Alleluia
Give thanks to the Risen Lord
Alleluia, Alleluia, give praise to his name.

Gospel   *Luke 10:25-28*

A teacher of the Law came up and tried to trap Jesus. "Teacher," he asked, "what must I do to receive eternal life?" Jesus answered him, "What do the Scriptures say? How do you interpret them?" The man answered, "'Love the Lord your God with all your heart, with all your soul, with all your strength, and with all your mind'; and 'Love your neighbour as you love yourself.'" "You are right," Jesus replied; "do this and you will live."

This is the Gospel of the Lord.

R/. Praise to you Lord Jesus Christ.

Prayer of the Faithful

[Celebrant] God of our past, present and future hear our prayers.

R/. Protect us in your love.

That the Church and all its members will be blessed.

R/. Protect us in your love.

That our teachers and all who have helped and supported us in this school will be rewarded.

R/. Protect us in your love.

That we may continue to experience the excitement of learning.

R/. Protect us in your love.

That parents and families will know we love them.

R/. Protect us in your love.

That we will be happy in our new school(s)

R/. Protect us in your love.

That we will be courageous in showing love and compassion to all we meet.

R/. Protect us in your love.

That through the prayers of Mary our Mother and the patron/patroness of this school we will do whatever God tells us.

R/. Protect us in your love.

[Celebrant] Faithful God, we have known your loving care each day of our lives in this school hear our prayers through Christ our Lord.

R/. Amen.

■ LITURGY OF THE EUCHARIST

Preparation of the Altar and procession with the gifts   *Music*

Prayer over the Gifts

Lord, look on us with love at this time,
Accept the gifts we offer and help us to grow in Christian love.
We ask this through Jesus Christ our Lord.

R/. Amen.

Eucharistic Prayer

Eucharistic Prayer for Children I

Prayer after Communion

Lord, may this sacrament we have received keep us on the way that leads to you.
We ask this in the name of Jesus the Lord.

R/. Amen.

■ CONCLUDING RITES

Blessing

Dismissal

OCCASIONS

Recessional hymn

Awake from your slumber!
Arise from your sleep!
A new day is dawning
for all those who weep.
The people in darkness
have seen a great light.
The Lord of our longing
has conquered the night.

[Chorus]

Let us build the city of God.
May our tears be turned into dancing!
For the Lord, our light and our Love,
has turned the night into day!

We are sons of the morning;
we are daughters of day.
The one who has loved us
has brightened our way.
The Lord of all kindness
has called us to be
a light for his people
to set their hearts free.

[Chorus]

God is light; in him there is not darkness.
Let us walk in his light,
his children, one and all.
O comfort my people;
make gentle your words.
Proclaim to my city
the day of her birth.
O city of gladness,
now lift up your voice!
Proclaim the good tidings
that all may rejoice!

[Chorus]

[Celebration Hymnal for Everyone no.65]
© *1981 Daniel L. Schutte and New Dawn Music*

2 TEACHER'S NOTES

Background

WE MARK stages in our lives. A few years ago there were just birthday cards and sympathy cards. Now there are ones for all sorts of occasions: you can get cards for new babies, passing driving tests, new jobs, retirement. These are times for celebration. It is also important that we mark events in a Christian way with prayer. Leaving school is a time of passage. It is therefore a time to look back and to look forward. We know the past, we do not know the future, so we give thanks and we place our confidence in God for the present and for what is to come.

Central focus

At this we hear the word of God inviting us to constancy and to love; the Mass will be the source of our strength in the years ahead.

Readings

If we use the bible for reflection and prayer, we will always be able to find a text to suit our needs and occasions in our lives. Today we hear St Paul inviting his young church at Philippi to remain faithful to what he taught them. Jesus gives the primary commandment to love God and everybody else.

Offertory

Procession with symbols and gifts:
- ○ Each school leaver to bring a page (about 50 words) on which they have written what school has meant to them.
- ○ A banner with the word "Thanks."
- ○ A banner with the word "Sorry."
- ○ School Mission Statement.
- ○ Bread and wine.

Eucharistic Prayer

Eucharistic Prayer for Children I
Preface of the Holy Spirit.

The Preface always tells us why today we give thanks at Mass. Today it is for the gift of the Holy Spirit and for guidance in the future.

Acclamation	*Sung*
Memorial Acclamation	*Sung*
Great Amen	*Sung*
Communion	*Music*

Follow up

To forgive any distress we have suffered in school. To give thanks for received blessings.

3 CELEBRANT'S NOTES

Background

INTRODUCTION TO THE MASS

THERE are many rites of passage in life and one is surely leaving a school to move on to a new stage of education or life. It is a time for looking backwards in thanksgiving; for looking backwards in forgiveness; for looking forwards in hope and expectation.

Readings

The readings point to values for our lives. St Paul summarises what it should mean for us to be followers of Christ. The Gospel points to love, the supreme value for our lives.

Homily pointers

The homily should look backwards and forwards:

- ○ Recognise that some have painful memories of school, e.g. failures, bullying, broken friendships etc. We need to move on in life, often by forgiving.
- ○ Thanksgiving for so much: education, friendships, care from others, achievements in education, skills, cultural enrichment, broadening of vision, understanding of the world, etc.
- ○ Looking to the future; some will be apprehensive, some will be insecure, some will be disappointed, some eager, excited at a new phase of life.
- ○ God will be with them. We can apply the words of Jesus, "I have gone to prepare a place for you."

Communion reflection

Tell Jesus your deepest feelings about leaving this school.

Dismissal

God will be with you; will you be with God?

ANNIVERSARY OF SCHOOL

1 LITURGY

Opening hymn

Be still, for the presence of the Lord.
the Holy One is here.
Come, bow before Him now,
with reverence and fear.
In Him no sin is found,
we stand on holy ground.
Be still, for the presence of the Lord,
the Holy One is here.

Be still, for the glory of the Lord
is shining all around;
He burns with holy fire,
with splendour He is crowned.
How awesome is the sight,
our radiant King of Light!
Be still, for the glory of the Lord
is shining all around.

Be still, for the power of the Lord
is moving in this place,
He comes to cleanse and heal,
to minister His grace.
No work too hard for Him,
in faith receive from Him,
Be still, for the power of the Lord
is moving in this place.

[Celebration Hymnal for Everyone no.72]

© 1986 Thankyou Music / Administered by worshiptogether.com songs

■ INTRODUCTORY RITES

Greeting

Penitential Rite

Lord, you have blessed your people.
   R/. Lord have mercy.

Lord, you have given strength and courage.
   R/. Christ have mercy.

Lord, you have offered the way of truth and hope.
   R/. Lord have mercy.

Opening prayer

Faithful God, we praise and thank you as we recall the anniversary of this school to your service. May the power of your word and sacrament bring strength to all who teach, learn and gather here.
We ask this through our Lord Jesus Christ who lives and reigns with you and the Holy Spirit one God for ever and ever.
   R/. Amen.

■ LITURGY OF THE WORD

First Reading   Romans 12:6-8

We are to use our different gifts in accordance with the grace that God has given us. If our gift is to speak God's message, we should do it according to the faith that we have; if it is to teach, we should teach; if it is to encourage others, we should do so. Whoever shares with others should do it generously; whoever has authority should work hard; whoever shows kindness to others should do it cheerfully.

This is the Word of the Lord.
   R/. Thanks be to God.

Responsorial Psalm   *Psalm 118*

R/. Give thanks to the Lord, for he is good.

Give thanks to the Lord, because he is good;
his love is eternal.
Who can tell all the great things he has done?
Who can praise him enough?
Happy are those who obey his commands,
who always do what is right.

R/. Give thanks to the Lord, for he is good.

Remember me, Lord, when you help your
people;
Include me when you save them.
Let me see the prosperity of your people
And share in the happiness of your nation,
In the glad pride of those who belong to you.

R/. Give thanks to the Lord, for he is good.

Gospel Acclamation   *Sung*

Celtic Alleluia.

[Celebration Hymnal for Everyone no.410]

Gospel   *Luke 19:15-17*

Some people brought their babies to Jesus for
him to place his hands on them. The disciples
saw them and scolded them for doing so, but
Jesus called the children to him and said, "Let
the children come to me and do not stop them,
because the kingdom of God belongs to such as
these. Remember this! Whoever does not
receive the Kingdom of God like a child will
never enter it."

This is the Gospel of the Lord.

R/. Praise to you Lord Jesus Christ.

Prayer of the Faithful

[Celebrant] Generous Father, with thanksgiving
we pray

R/. Lord, bless our school.

That Jesus Christ and the teaching of his
Church may always be the centre of our school.

R/. Lord, bless our school.

That all who have generously contributed to
this school over the years be rewarded.

R/. Lord, bless our school.

That governors, teachers, priests and parents
will always work together for the good of this
school.

R/. Lord, bless our school.

That we may always have reason to be proud
of our school.

R/. Lord, bless our school.

That deceased members of this school
community may have eternal life.

R/. Lord, bless our school.

That through the prayers of Mary our Mother,
and .... the patron/patroness of this
school we may follow God's way.

R/. Lord, bless our school.

[Celebrant] Father of all goodness listen to our
prayers which we make through Jesus our
Teacher and Lord.

R/. Amen.

■ LITURGY OF THE EUCHARIST

Preparation of the Altar and procession with the gifts   *Music*

Prayer over the Gifts

Lord, accept our gifts and gratitude.
May our sharing in this sacrament help us to
live as instruments of your love.
We ask this through Christ our Lord.

R/. Amen.

Eucharistic Prayer
"Jesus the Way to the Father"

We give thanks today that the Father has
given us Jesus as the Way, the Truth and the
Life.

Prayer after Communion

All-powerful God, may this holy meal help
and support us as we seek to follow Christ
our Teacher. We ask this in the name of
Jesus the Lord.

R/. Amen.

■ CONCLUDING RITES

Blessing

Dismissal

Recessional hymn

On this school your blessing, Lord;
on this school your grace bestow.
On this school your blessing, Lord;
may it come and never go.
Bringing peace and joy and happiness,
bringing love that knows no end.
On this school your blessing, Lord;
on this school your blessing send.

On this school your loving, Lord;
may it overflow each day.
On this school your loving, Lord;
may it come and with us stay.
Drawing us in love and unity
by the love received from you.
On this school your loving, Lord;
may it come each day anew.

On this school your giving, Lord;
may it turn and ever flow.
On this school your giving, Lord;
on this school your wealth bestow.
Filling all our hopes and wishes, Lord,
in the way you know is best.
On this school your giving, Lord;
may it come and with us rest.

On this school your calling, Lord;
may it come to us each day.
On this school your calling, Lord;
may it come to lead the way.
Filling us with nobler yearnings, Lord,
calling us to live in you.
On this school your calling, Lord;
may it come each day anew.

*[Celebration Hymnal for Everyone no.576
with change of "house" to "school"]*

© *McCrimmmon Publishing Co., Ltd.*

② TEACHER'S NOTES

Background

A SCHOOL is more than building and furniture. It is above all people. An anniversary is a time for looking back and giving thanks. There are many people that we should remember: the founders of the school who saw a need in this area.

There have been many pupils and teachers, many people have worked here. There are others who have made a great contribution to the school: parents and governors, clergy and benefactors, those who have been interested in the school and supported it in any way.

Central focus

The Mass is the source and summit of our lives. To this Mass we bring all those things for which we should be thanks, all the people who have been involved in the school.

Readings

The first reading tells of the various gifts that the Holy Spirit gives to the Church. The Gospel shows us Jesus' special care for children.

Offertory

Procession with symbols and gifts:

- ○ Admissions register/logbook.
- ○ Banner with date of foundation.
- ○ Names of founder.
- ○ Historical documents, photographs.
- ○ Commemorative plaque, icon, or tree sapling to mark the anniversary.
- ○ Bread and wine.

Eucharistic Prayer

"Jesus the Way to the Father"

We give thanks today that the Father has given us Jesus as the Way, the Truth and the Life.

Acclamation   *Sung*

Memorial Acclamation   *Sung*

Great Amen   *Sung*

Follow up

Continue to find our more about the school and to take pride in it; how can I contribute more to its life?

3 CELEBRANT'S NOTES

Background

INTRODUCTION TO THE MASS

IN OUR CULTURE we mark anniversaries of events: achievements and disasters. It is important to remember significant events of the past, to see how they touch the present. As Christians we seek to celebrate the anniversary with God's eyes. The celebration of a school anniversary is an occasion of pride and thanksgiving to God. It is also a time to remember the very many people who have contributed to it: pupils, teachers, staff, parents, the bishop of the diocese, priests and religious, inspectors, benefactors, local and central government and perhaps politicians and voluntary bodies. There may be special achievements to mark, or even tragedies or failures that should be recalled. All are to be brought to God in the Mass.

Readings

The first reading tells us of the many gifts or charisms that the Holy Spirit gives to the Church. As we listen we can recall the gifted people we have met in the school and observe our own gifts. Jesus is shown in the Gospel in his love and care for children.

Homily pointers

The complex reality which is any anniversary may be brought out by considering in the light of the New Testament all that has made up the school.

- ❍ The vision and courage those who founded the school.
- ❍ The love and dedication of those who have served it.
- ❍ The lives of pupils.
- ❍ How God sees what we consider to be success or failure.
- ❍ Blessings of the past.
- ❍ How to cope with lack of success
- ❍ How good people have been to the school.

Communion reflection

Ask Jesus to be good to those in the school who have helped me.

Dismissal

The dismissal at Mass is: Go in peace to love and serve the Lord. Our school is a place to love and serve the Lord.

[Thanks to those who prepared the liturgy and participated in it.]

INSPECTION TIME

1 LITURGY

Opening hymn

If God is for us, who can be against,
if the Spirit of God has set us free?

I know that nothing in this world
can ever take us from his love.

[Chorus]

Nothing can take us from his love,
poured out in Jesus, the Lord.

[Chorus]

And nothing present or to come
can ever take us from his love.

[Chorus]

I know that neither death not life
can ever take us from his love.

[Celebration Hymnal for Everyone, no.295]

© 1976 John B. Foley SJ and New Dawn Music

▥ INTRODUCTORY RITES

Greeting

Penitential Rite

Lord Jesus you call us continually to renewal and improvement.

R/. Lord have mercy.

Lord Jesus you teach us your way.

R/. Christ have mercy.

Lord Jesus you raise us up to new life.

R/. Lord have mercy.

Opening prayer

God, our Father and Protector help us to use our talents wisely. Send your Spirit upon our school that we may be well and peaceful in these days.
We ask this through our Lord Jesus Christ your Son who lives and reigns with you and the same Holy Spirit, one God for ever and ever.

R/. Amen.

▥ LITURGY OF THE WORD

First Reading

1 Corinthians 4:1-6
(paraphrased)

Paul wrote to the Corinthians: "Now, I am not at all concerned about being judged by you, or by any human standard; I don't even pass judgement on myself. My conscience is clear. But that does not prove that I am really all right. It is the Lord who passes judgement on me. Final judgement must wait on the Lord, who will bring to light everything, good and bad. Then all will receive from God the praise they deserve."

This is the Word of the Lord.

R/. Thanks be to God.

Responsorial Psalm

Song based on Isaiah 40

R/. Like a shepherd he feeds his flock
and gathers the lambs in his arms,
holding them carefully close to his heart,
leading them home.

Say to the cities of Judah;
'Prepare the way of the Lord'
Go to the mountain-top, lift your voice:
Jerusalem, here is your God.

R/. Like a shepherd...

I myself will shepherd them,
for others have led them astray.
The lost I will rescue and heal their wounds
and pasture them, giving them rest.

R/. Like a shepherd...

Come unto me
if you are heavily burdened,
and take my yoke upon your shoulders.
I will give you rest.

R/. Like a shepherd...

[Celebration Hymnal no.369]
© 1976 Robert J. Dufford SJ and New Dawn Music.

Gospel Acclamation

Alleluia

Alleluia, alleluia
Teach me your ways
that I may walk in your paths.
Alleluia.

Gospel   *Luke 13:22-24.29-30*

Jesus went through towns and villages, teaching the people and making his way towards Jerusalem. Someone asked him, "Sir, will just a few people be saved?" Jesus answered them, "Do your best to go in through the narrow door; because many people will surely try to go in but will not be able. People will come from the east and the west, from the north and the south, and sit down at the feast in the Kingdom of God. Then those who are now last will be first, and those who are now first will be last."

This is the Gospel of the Lord.

R/. Praise to you, Lord Jesus Christ.

Prayer of the Faithful

[Celebrant] The Holy Spirit is our Helper and Guide. We ask the blessing of the Spirit on our school.

R/. Come Holy Spirit.

For a vision of Catholic education in our country.

R/. Come Holy Spirit.

For the head teacher and deputy head teacher.

R/. Come Holy Spirit.

For teachers, teaching assistants and staff.

R/. Come Holy Spirit.

For all the pupils in this school.

R/. Come Holy Spirit.

For all the inspectors and their decisions.

R/. Come Holy Spirit.

For our school governors and all who work for the good of this school.

R/. Come Holy Spirit.

[Celebrant] God of wisdom listen to our prayers which we make through Christ our Lord.

R/. Amen.

■ LITURGY OF THE EUCHARIST

Preparation of the Altar and procession with the Gifts   *Music*

Prayer over the Gifts

Lord, may these gifts we offer increase our love for you and bring down your Spirit upon us.
We ask this through Christ our Lord.

R/. Amen.

Eucharistic Prayer
Masses for Children b) "God guides the Church on the Way of Salvation."

The Preface and Eucharistic Prayer invites us today to contemplate God's guidance on our journey.

Prayer after Communion

Lord, inspire us now and always by the gift of the Eucharist. May it guide and direct us in all that we do.
We ask this in the name of Jesus the Lord.

R/. Amen.

OCCASIONS

■ CONCLUDING RITES

Blessing

Dismissal

Recessional hymn

Sing it in the valleys,
shout it from the mountain tops;
Jesus came to save us,
and his saving never stops.
He is King of Kings,
and new life he brings,
sing it in the valleys,
shout it from the mountain tops, (Oh!)
shout it from the mountain tops.

Jesus you are by my side,
you take all my fears.
If I only come to you,
you will heal the pain of years.

[Chorus]

You have not deserted me,
though I go astray.
Jesus take me in your arms,
help me walk with you today.

[Chorus]

Jesus, you are living now,
Jesus, I believe.
Jesus, take me, heart and soul,
Yours alone I want to be.

[Chorus]

[Celebration Hymnal for Everyone no.648]

© 1983 Michael J. Anderson / Administered by Kevin Mayhew Ltd. Used by agreement.

2 TEACHER'S NOTES

Background

INSPECTION TIME is not easy; it is an anxious time for staff and pupils. What is needed is only that we all do our best. Everyone wants the school to be better and a happy place. Not everything will be inspected: there are very important educational values that cannot be inspected, like friendship, respect, collaboration, justice, compassion and kindness. In this week we want to show off our school; we want it to be a place that Jesus would be proud of.

Central focus

The key Christian values are all in the Eucharist. We celebrate this Eucharist to ask for the help we need. We also offer our school to God and invite the Holy Spirit to come upon us.

Readings

The two readings from St Paul and from the Gospel show us that God sees things differently from us. In the end it is God's judgement that counts. He does not expect more from us than the best we can do.

Offertory

Procession with symbols and gifts:

- ○ Mission statement.
- ○ Bible representing Jesus the Teacher.
- ○ Curriculum programmes/policies.
- ○ Candle with name of school and the inspectors.
- ○ Banner, "Come Holy Spirit."
- ○ Bread and wine.

Eucharistic Prayer

Masses for Children b) "God guides the Church on the Way of Salvation."

The Preface and Eucharistic Prayer invites us today to contemplate God's guidance on our journey.

Acclamation	*Sung*
Memorial Acclamation	*Sung*
Great Amen	*Sung*
Communion	*Music*

Follow up

Look out to care for each other in this week; we are all on display; God is looking on.

---

3 CELEBRANT'S NOTES

Background

INTRODUCTION TO THE MASS

I NSPECTION TIME is anxious for everybody. Class goes on, but somehow differently and there is a sense of unease. The whole point of inspection is to improve; a dentist looks into our mouth to see if everything is good inside. The result may be some discomfort, but it is worth it when we are assured that our teeth are fine. To have a Mass at this time is to allow the whole event to be brought under the word of God and to focus not on the tension of inspection, but on wider values of our lives in the school.

Readings

The readings set a new horizon, a wider perspective. Paul tells the Corinthians who were very critical of him and of other people,

that the true judgment is God's. We should think that these days are ones for God to inspect our school. The Gospel points out that the right way is often the more difficult way. But the rewards for living under the Gospel are without price.

Homily pointers

Some of the following points may be useful to open up a wider perspective:

- ❍ Prayer for our teachers; they can be weak and vulnerable too.
- ❍ Respect and prayer for our fellow pupils.
- ❍ We never know what burdens another pupil may be carrying on a particular day.
- ❍ Give thanks for those values of the school that are not just books and academics, such as friendship, respect, compassion, kindness, pride in our school, cooperation, team spirit.
- ❍ Seeing inspection as positive; it will improve the school.
- ❍ The true judgement belongs to God: we need to wonder what is God pleased with in our school, and what God would like us to change.
- ❍ Attitudes of peace, mutual understanding, responsibility and enjoyment will help us through.
- ❍ We need to be positive and thankful about ourselves and others.
- ❍ Remember the Holy Spirit whom invoke to guide us through these days.

Communion reflection

Tell Jesus how you feel about the inspection; ask for his help for our school.

Dismissal

Positive attitudes are important at this time and for the rest of the school year and indeed the rest of life.

[Thanks to those who prepared the liturgy and participated in it.]

RETIREMENT

1 LITURGY

Opening hymn

Though the mountains may fall,
and the hills turn to dust,
Yet the love of the Lord will stand
as a shelter for all who will call on his name.
Sing the praise and the glory of God.

[Celebration Hymnal for Everyone no.739]

© 1975 Daniel L. Schutte and New Dawn Music

■ INTRODUCTORY RITES

Greeting

Penitential Rite

Lord Jesus, you reward those who do good
to others.

R/. Lord have mercy.

Lord Jesus, you draw us into renewal of life.

R/. Christ have mercy.

Lord Jesus, you are a light for our path.

R/. Lord have mercy.

Opening prayer

Gentle Creator God, we give thanks for the
faithful service to the school of_____.
May we continue to be filled with the gift of
your Spirit and support and encourage each
other as we work for your glory. We ask this
through our Lord Jesus Christ your Son who
lives and reigns with you in the unity of the
Holy Spirit, one God, for ever and ever.

R/. Amen.

■ LITURGY OF THE WORD

First Reading
2 Timothy 4:5-8

You must perform your whole duty as a servant
of God. As for me, the hour has come for me
to be sacrificed; the time is here for me to
leave this life. I have done my best in the race,
I have run the full distance, and I have kept
the faith. And now there is waiting for me the
victory prize of being put right with God, which
the Lord, the righteous Judge, will give me on
that Day – and not only me, but to all those
who wait with love for him to appear.
This is the Word of the Lord.

R/. Thanks be to God.

Responsorial Psalm
Luke 1:46-55

[Hymns Old and New 661)

*R/. The Lord has done marvels for me:
Holy is his name.*

or

R/. My soul rejoices in my God.

My soul glorifies the Lord,
My spirit rejoices in God, my Saviour.

R/.

He looks on his servant in her nothingness;
Henceforth all ages will call me blessed.

R/.

The almighty works marvels for me.
Holy his name!

R/.

His mercy is from age to age,
On those who fear him.

R/.

He puts forth his arm in strength
And scatters the proud-hearted.

R/.

He casts the mighty from their thrones
And raises the lowly.

R/.

Gospel Acclamation
Sung

Alleluia, Alleluia,
I will be with you always
Alleluia, Alleluia.

Gospel
John 17:1.3-5

Jesus looked up to heaven and said "Father, the hour has come. Give glory to your Son, so that the Son may give glory to you. Eternal life means knowing you, the only true God, and knowing Jesus Christ whom you sent. I have shown your glory on earth; I have finished the work you gave me to do. Father! Give me the glory in your presence now, the same glory I had with you before the world was made."

This is the Gospel of the Lord.

R/. Praise to you, Lord Jesus Christ.

Prayer of the Faithful

[Celebrant] Source of all blessings we turn to you and pray:

R/. Generous God, bless us.

For the needs of our Church and our world today.

R/. Generous God, bless us.

For those who contribute to the mission of education.

R/. Generous God, bless us.

For_____ who retires from this school that he/she will be rewarded for his/her dedicated service.

R/. Generous God, bless us.

For your continued inspiration and blessing on this school community.

R/. Generous God, hear us.

That through the prayers of Mary and the patron/patroness of this school we may proclaim the Good News always.

R/. Generous God, hear us.

[Celebrant] Loving God, hear our prayers and continue to help us in our needs, through Christ our Lord.

R/. Amen.

■ LITURGY OF THE EUCHARIST

Preparation of the Altar and procession with the Gifts
Music

Prayer over the Gifts

Lord, look with love on our service. Accept the gifts we bring and help us grow in Christian love. We ask this in the name of Jesus the Lord.

R/. Amen.

Eucharistic Prayer

Eucharistic Prayers for various Occasions D: "Jesus the Compassion of God."

We give thanks for the compassion of Jesus; we see ourselves imitating this.

Prayer after Communion

Lord, you have nourished us with the bread of life. Help us to continue to serve and thank you by lives of faithful service.
We ask this in the name of Jesus the Lord.

R/. Amen.

■ CONCLUDING RITES

Blessing

Dismissal

Recessional hymn

"I will be with you"

[Celebration Hymnal for Everyone no.289]

2 TEACHER'S NOTES

Background

OUR SCHOOL is a community and each has a role which is significant. Everyone comes together to form a single tapestry of many colours. We do not always appreciate the small things that need to be done to make our time here pleasant.

It is often said that the best things said about a person is when they die. We have an opportunity today to say thanks for what we all have received.

Central focus

All our lives are to be brought into the Eucharist. Today we bring to the Lord the contribution to our school of _____.
We give thanks to God for this person and we ask God's future blessing on him/her.

Readings

The two readings are about people looking back over their lives. Paul is shown as an old man thanking God for remaining faithful.
The Gospel gives us the thoughts of Jesus just before his death. In his prayer to the Father he prays for his disciples whom he is temporally leaving.

Offertory

Procession with symbols and gifts:

○ Symbols associated with person retiring (e.g. keys, tools, books, food).
○ Card or Book of memories signed by school staff, letters of appreciation.
○ Gift.
○ Photographs with retiring person.
○ Flowers.
○ Bread and wine.

Eucharistic Prayer

Eucharistic Prayers for Various Occasions D: "Jesus the Compassion of God."

We give thanks for the compassion of Jesus; we see ourselves imitating this.

Acclamation	*Sung*
Memorial Acclamation	*Sung*
Great Amen	*Sung*
Communion	*Music*

Follow up

We all contribute to the spirit of the school. We should constantly show appreciation and thanks.

3 CELEBRANT'S NOTES

Background

INTRODUCTION TO THE MASS

WE ALL EXPERIENCE LIFE as comings and goings; people are around us, and then they are not. Life goes on. A retirement is an occasion of a person moving on, and of the school remembering their contribution and thanking them. It can be a time to look more closely at how the school operates and see how much we take for granted. Classes don't prepare themselves, floors are not self-cleaning, food doesn't cook itself, weeds do not die off by themselves, decisions have to be made by someone. Above all, the values and the ethos of the school are the combined work of everybody, pupils and staff. No one person can by themselves make a school a happy place where pupils are content to learn; rather it is a co-operative effort.

Readings

Shortly before their deaths, Paul and Jesus look back: Paul to give thanks for having continued the race and kept faith; Jesus is concerned with those whom he is leaving behind.

Homily pointers

A focus on the contribution of many people to the life of the school might be a framework for thanks to the person retiring:

○ The school a community where each has a part to play.
○ Everybody must be committed to the ethos of the school as laid down in the Mission Statement.
○ Faithfulness to duty.
○ The importance of showing appreciation and thanks to people, not just when they retire (or die!).
○ Thanks for the contribution of the retiree.

Communion reflection

Ask Jesus to bless the person retiring.

Dismissal

Remember to affirm and encourage others – pupils and staff – frequently.

[Thanks to those who prepared the liturgy and participated in it.]

LOCAL OR NATIONAL TRAGEDY

1 LITURGY

Opening hymn

Do not be afraid for I have redeemed you.
I have called you by your name;
your are mine.

When you walk through the waters
I'll be with you
You will never sink beneath the waves.

[Chorus]

You are mine, O my child,
I am your father
And I love you with a perfect love.

[Chorus]

[Celebration Hymnal for Everyone, no.147]
© 1978 Kevin Mayhew Ltd. Reproduced by permission from Hymns Old & New

▒ INTRODUCTORY RITES

Greeting

Penitential Rite

Lord, you call us to faith.
R/. Lord have mercy.

Lord, you offer us hope.
R/. Christ have mercy.

Lord, you restore our peace.
R/. Lord have mercy.

Opening prayer

Merciful Father, hear our prayers and console all who mourn especially as a result of this Local/National tragedy.
Make our faith strong and help us to trust in your promise of eternal life.
We ask this through our Lord Jesus Christ your Son who lives and reigns with you and the Holy Spirit one God for ever and ever.
R/. Amen.

▒ LITURGY OF THE WORD

First Reading   *Isaiah 25:6-9*

Here on Mount Zion the Lord Almighty will prepare a banquet for all the nations of the world – a banquet of the richest food and the finest wine. Here he will suddenly remove the cloud of sorrow that has been hanging over all over the nations. The Sovereign Lord will destroy death for ever! He will wipe away the tears from everyone's eyes and take away the disgrace his people have suffered throughout the world. The Lord himself has spoken! When it happens, everyone will say, "He is our God! We have put our trust in him, and he has rescued us. He is the Lord! We have put our trust in him, and now we are happy and joyful because he has saved us."

This is the word of the Lord.
R/. Thanks be to God.

Responsorial Psalm

Song based on Isaiah 40

R/. Like a shepherd he feeds his flock
and gathers the lambs in his arms,
holding them carefully close to his heart,
leading them home.

Say to the cities of Judah:
'Prepare the way of the Lord.'
Go to the mountain-top, lift your voice:
Jerusalem, here is your God.
R/.

I myself will shepherd them,
for others have led them astray.
The lost I will rescue and heal their wounds
and pasture them, giving them rest.
R/.

Come unto me
if you are heavily burdened,
and take my yoke upon your shoulders.
I will give you rest.
R/.

[Celebration Hymnal for Everyone no.369]
© 1976 Robert J. Dufford SJ and New Dawn Music

Gospel Acclamation *Sung*

Alleluia, alleluia, alleluia!
"I am the way the truth and the life"
says the Lord.
"No one can come to the Father except
through me."
Alleluia!

Gospel *Matthew 11: 25-30*

At that time Jesus said, "Father, Lord of heaven and earth! I thank you because you have shown to the unlearned what you have hidden from the wise and learned. Yes, Father this was how you wanted it to happen. My Father has given me all things. No one knows the Son except the Father, no one knows the Father except the Son and those to whom the Son chooses to reveal him. Come to me, all of you who are tired from carrying heavy loads, and I will give you rest. Take my yoke and put it on you, and learn from me, because I am gentle and humble in spirit; and you will find rest. For the yoke I will give you is easy, and the load I will put on you is light."

This is the Gospel of the Lord.

R/. Praise to you, Lord Jesus Christ.

Prayer of the Faithful

[Celebrant] Jesus said to his disciples:
"Come to me all you who are overburdened and I will give you rest". Let us pray to him:

R/. You are the way, the truth and the life.

That the Church may continue to be a sign of God's tender compassion for all.

R/. You are the way, the truth and the life.

That our faith may be strengthened at this time.

R/. You are the way, the truth and the life.

That all who have died in this tragedy will enjoy happiness for ever.

R/. You are the way, the truth and the life.

That those injured may be restored to health.

R/. You are the way, the truth and the life.

That relief workers may be kept safe and made strong.

R/. You are the way, the truth and the life.

That all who mourn the passing of their loved ones will be comforted.

R/. You are the way, the truth and the life.

That we will all continue to live good lives.

R/. You are the way, the truth and the life.

[Celebrant] God of the living and the dead we entrust to your gracious keeping all who have died. May they enjoy forever your everlasting love and peace.

R/. Amen.

■ LITURGY OF THE EUCHARIST

Preparation of the altar and procession with the Gifts *Music*

Prayer over the Gifts

Lord, we are united in this sacrament by the love of Christ. Accept these gifts and receive our brother and sisters into the glory of your Son, who is Lord forever and ever.

R/. Amen.

Eucharistic Prayer
Eucharistic Prayer for Children III
Outside the Easter Season.

As we come to the Father we are aware of joys and sorrows that we can bring.

Prayer after Communion

Lord God, may the death and resurrection of Christ which we celebrate in this Eucharist, bring healing the injured [and bring all who have died in this tragedy to the peace and joy of your eternal home].
We ask this in name of Jesus the Lord.

R/. Amen.

OCCASIONS

■ CONCLUDING RITES

Blessing

Dismissal

Recessional hymn

Amazing grace! How sweet the sound
that saved a wretch like me.
I once was lost but now I'm found,
was blind, but now I see.

'Twas grace that taught my heart to fear,
and grace my fears relieved.
How precious did that grace appear
the hour I first believed.

Through many dangers, toils and snares
I have already come.
'Tis grace hath brought me safe thus far,
and grace will lead me home.

The Lord has promised good to me;
his word my hope secures.
He will my shield and portion be
as long as life endures.

[Celebration Hymnal for Everyone no.40]

2 TEACHER'S NOTES

Background

AT A TIME OF TRAGEDY there is much need for prayer. We pray for those who have died that they may quickly be brought to home with God. We pray for those injured, that they be healed and strengthened. We pray for affected relatives. We also need to pray for ourselves, as we can all react differently, and our faith may need strengthening. Facing tragedy is a major step in the whole process of maturation.

Central focus

It is in the Eucharist that we seek to find meaning and comfort in distress. We bring our confused, angry or depressed selves to the Paschal Mystery of Jesus. We bring also those who have suffered in their various needs.

Readings

The two readings are words of comfort from God. The first is a promise of ultimate restoration when all sorrow will have passed. The Gospel is more immediate: it is Jesus offering comfort and support to those who find life burdensome.

Offertory

Procession with symbols and gifts:

○ Rose or other petals
   [if appropriate: money to be sent to disaster area].
○ Map of country or globe with indication of place to show solidarity.
○ Newspaper headlines.
○ Banner with appropriate quotation from Church and political leaders, from media.
○ Bread and wine

Eucharistic Prayer
Eucharistic Prayer for Children III
Outside the Easter Season.

As we come to the Father we are aware of joys and sorrows that we can bring.

Acclamation	*Sung*
Memorial Acclamation	*Sung*
Great Amen	*Sung*
Communion	*Music*

Follow up

Ongoing prayer for victims in the days and weeks ahead.

3 CELEBRANT'S NOTES

Background

INTRODUCTION TO THE MASS

THERE WILL BE A RANGE of reactions in the school to tragedies: some become deeply upset, others do not seem to care. Some can find their faith in a loving God tested very deeply. The liturgy in this case can be educational. The word of God and the homily can seek to place the disaster in perspective. We can bring our distress and numb pain to God by offering them along with Christ's sacrifice present on the altar. Jesus who suffered desolation on the Cross heals and redeems the darkness that can enfold us.

Readings

The first reading looks to the future. God's people are in distress, but God promises a time of restoration when grief and sorrow will be taken away. The fullness of this distant prophecy is still awaited; God will bring us home where there will be no more tears. Jesus offers comfort to those who feel oppressed and overburdened.

Homily pointers

The homily might seek to explore God's ways and place the tragedy in a Christian perspective:

○ God's ways not our ways.
○ The cry of "why O Lord?" – that may not seem to have an answer.
○ God gives us comfort and strength rather than answers.
○ Tragedy calls forth various prayers: for those who have died; for the injured, for relatives and friends, for those who are engaged in relief work. Such prayer opens us up out of narrow selfishness. We need at times to put our worries and pains in perspective.
○ Our future home with God.

Communion reflection

Talk to Jesus about the tragedy: tell him how you feel and ask his help for those affected.

Dismissal

Keep up prayer for those affected by the tragedy.

[Thanks to those who prepared the liturgy and participated in it.]

DEATH OF A PUPIL

1 LITURGY

Opening hymn

You shall cross the barren deserts,
but you shall not die of thirst.
You shall wander far in safety
though you do not know the way.
You shall speak your words to foreign men
and they will understand.
You shall see the face of God and live.

Be not afraid, I go before you always.
Come, follow me, and I will give you rest.

If you pass through raging waters in the sea,
you shall not drown.
If you walk amid the burning flames,
you shall not be harmed.
If you stand before the pow'r of hell
and death is at your side,
know that I am with you through it all.

[Chorus]

Blessed are your poor,
for the kingdom shall be theirs.
Blest are you that weep and mourn,
for one day you shall laugh.
And if wicked men insult and hate you
all because of me,
blessed, blessed are you!

[Chorus]

[Celebration Hymnal for Everyone no.830]
© 1975/1978 Robert J. Dufford and New Dawn Music

■ INTRODUCTORY RITES

Greeting

Penitential Rite

You are the way to the Father.
R/. Lord have mercy.

You prepare a place for us and return to take us home.
R/. Christ have mercy.

You promised that all who believe in your will never die.
R/. Lord have mercy.

Opening prayer

Loving Father, hear our prayers and comfort us as we mourn the passing of _____.
Help us to know your will, accept and follow it with courage and trust. We ask this through our Lord Jesus Christ who lives and reigns with you and the Holy Spirit one God for ever and ever.
R/. Amen.

■ LITURGY OF THE WORD

First Reading   *1 Thessalonians 4:13-14.18*

Brothers and sisters, we want you to know the truth about those who have died, so that you will not be sad, as are those who have no hope. We believe that Jesus died and rose again, and so we believe that God will take back with Jesus those who have died believing in him. So then encourage one another with these words.

This is the Word of the Lord.
R/. Thanks be to God.

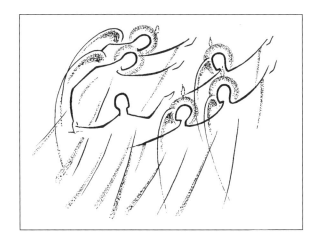

Responsorial Psalm Psalm 23

> *R/. Cast your cares on the Lord.*

The Lord is my shepherd;
I have everything that I need.
He gives me new strength,
he guides me in the right paths.

> *R/. Cast your cares on the Lord.*

I know that your goodness and love
will be with me all my life.
And your house will be my home
as long as I live.

> *R/. Cast your cares on the Lord.*

Gospel Acclamation Sung

Alleluia, Alleluia, Alleluia!
Come to me all you who are burdened,
and I will refresh you, says the Lord.
Alleluia!

Gospel John 11: 21-27

Martha said to Jesus, "If you had been here, Lord, my brother would not have died! But I know that even now God will give you whatever you ask him for." "Your brother will rise to life," Jesus told her. "I know," she replied, "that he will rise to life on the last day." Jesus said to her, "I am the resurrection and the life. Whoever believes in me will live, even though he dies; and whoever lives and believes in me will never die. Do you believe this?" "Yes, Lord!" She answered. "I do believe that you are the Messiah, the Son of God, who was to come into the world."

This is the Gospel of the Lord.

> *R/. Praise to you, Lord Jesus Christ.*

Prayer of the Faithful

[Celebrant] We turn to our loving Father and pray:

> *R/. Be our strength Lord at this time.*

That our faith may not fail.

> *R/. Be our strength Lord at this time.*

That the family of _____ may be comforted at this time.

> *R/. Be our strength Lord at this time.*

That the friends of _____ may support one another.

> *R/. Be our strength Lord at this time.*

That this death may strengthen bonds in the community.

> *R/. Be our strength Lord at this time.*

That the Lord may bring _____ to his home in heaven.

> *R/. Be our strength Lord at this time.*

[Celebrant] Lord look upon our distress and hear our prayers, spoken and unspoken, which we make through Christ our Lord.

> *R/. Amen.*

■ LITURGY OF THE EUCHARIST

Preparation of the altar and procession with the Gifts Music

Prayer over the Gifts

Lord, accept our offering. May it console and renew us, and lead us to our eternal reward. We ask this through Christ our Lord.

> *R/. Amen.*

Eucharistic Prayer
Eucharistic Prayer for Children II.
Preface of Christian Death II.

We give thanks today because through Jesus Christ death is not the end.

Prayer after Communion

Lord you strengthen us with food from heaven. Keep us all united in your love until we are reunited with you in glory.
We ask this in the name of Jesus the Lord.

R/. Amen.

■ CONCLUDING RITES

Blessing

Dismissal

Recessional hymn

*Like a shepherd he feeds his flock
and gathers the lambs in his arms,
holding them carefully close to his heart,
leading them home.*

Say to the cities of Judah:
'Prepare the way of the Lord.'
Go to the mountain-top, lift your voice:
Jerusalem, here is your God.

[Chorus]

I myself will shepherd them,
for others have led them astray.
The lost I will rescue and heal their wounds
and pasture them, giving them rest.

[Chorus]

Come unto me
if you are heavily burdened,
and take my yoke upon your shoulders.
I will give you rest.

[Celebration Hymnal for Everyone no.369]

© 1976 Robert J. Dufford and New Dawn Music

② TEACHER'S NOTES

Background

THE WORD that is in all our minds is surely, "Why?" There are no answers that will take away our pain, but there are thoughts that will give us strength. The Christian vision of death is that of going home, going to Jesus who has already gone to prepare a place for us. There are three thoughts that we could bring to Mass:

Our sorrow
Our thanks for having known_____
Our prayer for _____, friends and family.

Central focus

The Mass which celebrates the death and rising of Jesus is where we need to look.
He has died that we might live eternally.
The Mass is to strengthen our hope.

Readings

Paul is comforting the Thessalonians, assuring them that the dead will rise again.
Their sorrow, he says, is not to be like the sadness of those who have no hope.
The Gospel shows Martha and Jesus talking about the death of her brother, a friend of Jesus.

Offertory

Procession with symbols and gifts:

- ❍ Photograph.
- ❍ Candle with name of pupil.
- ❍ A personal memento of pupil e.g. exercise book, tie, badge.
- ❍ A flower or rose petals to be left on grave.
- ❍ Book of condolences.
- ❍ Bread and Wine.

Eucharistic Prayer

Eucharistic Prayer for Children II.
Preface of Christian Death II.

We give thanks today because through Jesus Christ death is not the end.

Sanctus Acclamation	*Sung*
Memorial Acclamation	*Sung*
Great Amen	*Sung*
Communion	*Music*

Follow up

Practical support of those most distressed by this death.
Learn the prayer, "Eternal rest grant to the dead O Lord. May they rest in peace."

③ CELEBRANT'S NOTES

Background

INTRODUCTION TO MASS

THE DEATH OF A PUPIL will give rise to a huge range of reactions in the school: from guilt and profound grief to callous disinterest. Some pupils have so much pain and distress in their own families and surroundings that they just cannot take on board other people's suffering. The task is to give a Christian response to a school death. Looking at the reality and avoiding any facile generalisations like "It's all God's will," which though true might at this time be singularly unhelpful. Much better is pointing to the strength that God can give, and to future reunion in God.

Readings

The first reading gives Paul's teaching to the Thessalonians as they wrestled with grief. He knows that they mourn, but their sorrow is not to be like that of the pagans who do not have hope. The Gospel is a conversation between Jesus and Martha about the death of Lazarus who was a friend of Jesus and her brother. It looks to a life after death.

Homily pointers

The homily might take up the multifaceted ritual of Christian death:
- ◯ Death is not the end, we look forward to reunion.
- ◯ Remember and give thanks for the life of the dead pupil.
- ◯ Future resurrection: life with God, life with the saints, with our relatives and friends for ever.
- ◯ The unanswerable questions about suffering.
- ◯ We must all prepare for death by the way we live.
- ◯ Support for the family and friends of the dead pupil.
- ◯ Prayers for the dead.

Communion reflection

Talk to Jesus about the dead pupil and how you feel

Dismissal

Jesus is always with us.

MASS FOR A SUICIDE VICTIM

1 LITURGY

Opening hymn

I, the Lord of sea and sky,
I have heard my people cry
All who dwell in dark and sin
My hand will save.
I who made the stars of night,
I will make their darkness bright,
Who will bear my light to them?
Whom shall I send?

Here I am Lord. Is it I Lord?
I have heard you calling in the night.
I will go, Lord, if you lead me.
I will hold your people in my heart.

[Celebration Hymnal for Everyone no.285]

■ INTRODUCTORY RITES

Greeting

Penitential Rite

You are our Loving Shepherd.
  R/. Lord have mercy.

You lead us into peaceful pastures.
  R/. Christ have mercy.

You embrace us in a rainbow of mercy.
  R/. Lord have mercy.

Opening prayer

Compassionate Father, you have called
(name) from this life. Enfold him (her) in the
love and peace he (she) so desired.
We ask this through our Lord Jesus Christ,
your Son, who lives and reigns with you and
the Holy Spirit, one God, for ever and ever.
  R/. Amen.

■ LITURGY OF THE WORD

First Reading   *1 Thess. 4:13-14.18*

Brothers and sisters, we want you to know the
truth about those who have died, so that you
will not be sad, as are those who have no hope.
We believe that Jesus died and rose again, and
so we believe that God will take back with Jesus
those who have died believing in him. So then,
encourage one another with these words.

This is the word of the Lord.
  R/. Thanks be to God.

Responsorial Psalm

  *R/. Do not be afraid,
    for I have redeemed you.
    I have called you by your name;
    you are mine.*

When you walk through the waters
I'll be with you.
You will never sink beneath the waves.

  *R/. Do not be afraid,
    for I have redeemed you.
    I have called you by your name;
    you are mine.*

When the fear of loneliness is looming,
then remember I am at your side.

  *R/. Do not be afraid,
    for I have redeemed you.
    I have called you by your name;
    you are mine.*

You are mine, O my child; I am your Father,
and I love you with a perfect love.

  *R/. Do not be afraid,
    for I have redeemed you.
    I have called you by your name;
    you are mine.*

[Celebration Hymnal for Everyone no.147]

Gospel Acclamation *Sung*

Alleluia, Alleluia!
Come to me all you who labour and are
burdened and I will give you rest.
Alleluia.

Gospel *Matthew 11:28-30*

Jesus said, "Come to me, all of you who are tired
from carrying heavy loads, and I will give you
rest. Take my yoke and put it on you, and learn
from me, because I am gentle and humble in
spirit; and you will find rest. For the yoke I will
give you is easy, and the load I will put on you
is light."

This is the Gospel of the Lord.

R/. Praise to you Lord Jesus Christ

Prayer of the Faithful

[Celebrant] We turn to our Compassionate God
and pray:

R/. Lord let your face shine on us.

That our church will be a sign of your love and
compassion.

R/. Lord let your face shine on us.

That [N.] will know your embracing love and
peace.

R/. Lord let your face shine on us.

That the family of [N.] will be consoled and
strengthened at this time.

R/. Lord let your face shine on us.

That we may be life-affirming in our outlook.

R/. Lord let your face shine on us.

That we may look forward with hope and
courage.

R/. Lord let your face shine on us.

That this community and all of us present will
trust in your promises.

R/. Lord let your face shine on us.

[Celebrant] God of the living and the dead,
Comforter of all, listen to our prayers,
spoken and unspoken, which we make
through Christ our Lord.

R/. Amen.

■ LITURGY OF THE EUCHARIST

Preparation of the Altar and procession with the gifts *Music*

Prayer over Gifts

Lord we are united in this sacrament
by the love of Christ.
Accept these gifts and receive our
brother/sister into the glory of your Son,
who is Lord for ever and ever.

R/. Amen.

Eucharistic Prayer

Prayer after Communion

Lord God, may the death of Christ
which we celebrate in this Eucharist
bring (N.) and all who have died
into the peace of your eternal love.
We ask this in the name of Jesus the Lord.

R/. Amen.

■ CONCLUDING RITE

Blessing

Dismissal

Recessional hymn

"You shall cross the barren desert"

[Celebration Hymnal for Everyone no.830]

OCCASIONS

② TEACHER'S NOTES

Background

WHEN someone we love and is close to us dies we can be quite bewildered and ask the question "why?" If that person takes their own life and leaves us suddenly, we are usually devastated and search for reasons or clues as to why we did not recognise some signs that all was not well with this person. We can wear ourselves out with guilt. But the person who left us through the illness of suicide was so locked or imprisoned in their pain and darkness that our love and friendship could not reach them; the lonely act of suicide excluded family and friends. Perhaps they could not reach out for help? We do not understand fully how or what suicide victims suffer prior to their death: was it planned over a period, or was it an impulse, perhaps arising from panic and thus unplanned? Almost certainly they did not adequately consider the pain their act would cause to their family and friends. Today we are more conscious of illness that can lie behind suicide, but we must avoid glorifying it like the ancient Romans, who considered it honourable. One thing we are sure of is that God's love for the victim is far greater than ours even at its best. God can reach each person in whatever circumstance he or she finds themselves. So, we entrust them now to God's loving embrace. This liturgy is a commitment of the dead person to God; it is also a liturgy to help us who remain to cope with the devastation of suicide.

Central Focus

The Mass is a meeting place for all God's children. We join with all the saints already in glory and we pray for those who have died and may still need healing by the Lord. It is also a statement made solemnly in worship that we ourselves will look forward and support one another.

Readings

The first reading brings present the grounds for Christian hope. It is the death and resurrection of Jesus, we hope that the person who died had some remnant of hope and that the Lord will surround them with love and mercy.

The Gospel reading refers to our state. In our difficulties we need to turn to Jesus and have a relationship with him. In this way we can be protected from the onset of despair that can have such devastating consequences.

Offertory

Procession with symbols and gifts:

- ○ Bouquet of flowers.
- ○ Symbols of home and family life.
- ○ Baptismal candle.
- ○ Symbols of school life.
- ○ Symbols of sport / club interests.
- ○ Bread and wine which after the Consecration will unite heaven and earth.

Eucharistic Prayer

In the Eucharistic Prayer we unite with heaven and earth. We join with Mary and the saints in praying for the dead.

Sanctus Acclamation   *Sung*

Memorial Acclamation   *Sung*

Great Amen   *Sung*

Communion   *Sung*

Follow up

Thank God for the happy memories we have of [N.]

3 CELEBRANT'S NOTES

Background

INTRODUCTION TO MASS

A MASS at the time of suicide is one of the most difficult challenges for a celebrant. We are now much more aware of the various forms of psychiatric illness that underlie suicide, and predispose the person to think that there is no way out, when some event triggers the act of self-harm. We now think of God's love and mercy in these circumstances; we no longer indulge in stigmatising the victim, family or friends. A prominent politician has recently stated in parliament: "If we are to lead young people away from despair and hopelessness then they have to be given hope, vision and leadership." Suicide should not happen; it should never be glorified or spoken of in a way that might encourage copy-cat suicides. Without blaming the victim, we need to be aware of the harm, guilt and misery that suicide causes for family and friends. We must all contribute to society in a way that gives support to those who are ill or facing what they see as an impossible future.

Readings

St Paul tells the Thessalonians to have hope in the resurrection of Jesus. He tells his recent converts that death makes sense only when seen in the context of Jesus' own death. The Gospel shows us where to turn in our present sorrow now and in the future when we feel things closing in around us and we are plagued by thoughts that are increasingly more negative.

Homily pointers

○ God loves the dead person more than we do; we commit him/her to his mercy.
○ It is useless to ask "why" the person died.
○ We must be careful of guilt, of wondering "if only..." Maybe we could have done more, but the dead person became so isolated that it was difficult to know what was going on in their lives.
○ Remembering the person who has died; giving thanks for the gift the person was – life is a gift: it is to be cherished, but is fragile and needs to be nurtured, cared for and protected.
○ We need to be life-affirming in all our activities.
○ The need to strengthen one another and the victim's family over the next few weeks, months, years. This gives a focus that links in with the culture and values important to teenagers and young adults. It shows what those who are grieving can do: it is positive, forward looking and life-affirming.
○ It might be appropriate to recall the saying of Dietrich Bonhoeffer in a Nazi concentration camp when confronted with the thought of suicide: "Only God knows when we have reached the perfection he has planned for us." [Bonhoeffer himself was hanged shortly afterwards, indeed just three weeks before Hitler died.]
○ We should use language like "coping with the future" – "as we move on" – "as we continue with our lives."

Communion reflection

Thank the Lord for the gift of knowing the victim.
Ask for the grace for a strong and constant hope.

Dismissal

Leave aside depressing thoughts; look around with thanksgiving, recall good moments, memories to be treasured.

CLOSING OF THE SCHOOL YEAR

1 LITURGY

Opening hymn

Longing for light, we wait in darkness.
Longing for truth, we turn to you.
Make us your own, your holy people,
light for the world to see.

*Christ be our light! Shine in our hearts.
Shine through the darkness.
Christ be our light! Shine in your church
gathered today.*

Longing for peace, our world is troubled.
Longing for hope, many despair.
Your word alone has pow'r to save us.
make us your living voice.

[Chorus]

Longing for food, many are hungry.
Longing for water, many still thirst.
Make us your bread, broken for others,
shared until all are fed.

[Chorus]

Longing for shelter, many are homeless.
Longing for warmth, many are cold.
Make us your building, sheltering others,
walls made of living stone.

[Chorus]

Many the gifts, many the people,
many the hearts that yearn to belong.
let us be servants to one another,
making your kingdom come.

[Chorus]

*[Celebration Carols no.15]
© 1994 Bernadette Farrell. Published by OCP Publications.*

■ INTRODUCTORY RITES

Greeting

Penitential Rite

You come to teach us the way of love
 R/. Lord have mercy.

You taught us to forgive always.

R/. Christ have mercy.

You are with us always and everywhere.
 R/. Lord have mercy.

Opening prayer

Lord, help us to do your will as we come to
the end of this school year.
Nourish us with your word of life.
We ask this through our Lord Jesus Christ
your Son who lives and reigns with you and
the Holy Spirit, one God for ever and ever.
 R/. Amen.

■ LITURGY OF THE WORD

First Reading   Isaiah 63:7

I will tell of the Lord's unfailing love, I praise him
for all he has done for us. He has richly blessed
the people of Israel because of his mercy and
constant love.

This is the Word of the Lord.
 R/. Thanks be to God.

Responsorial Psalm

Collage of scripture texts

I will give thanks to you, my Lord.
You have answered my plea.
You have saved my soul from death.
You are my strength and my song.

*R/. Sing to the mountains, sing to the sea.
Raise your voices, lift your hearts.
This is the day the Lord has made.
Let all the earth rejoice.*

Holy, holy, holy Lord.
Heaven and earth are full of your glory.

*R/. Sing to the mountains, sing to the sea.
Raise your voices, lift your hearts.
This is the day the Lord has made.
Let all the earth rejoice.*

This is the day that the Lord has made.
Let us be glad and rejoice.
He has turned all death to life.
Sing of the glory of God.

R/. Sing to the mountains, sing to the sea.
Raise your voices, lift your hearts.
This is the day the Lord has made.
Let all the earth rejoice.

[Celebration Hymnal for Everyone no.657]
© 1975 Robert J. Dufford SJ and New Dawn Music

Gospel Acclamation   *Sung*

Alleluia, Alleluia!
This is the day the Lord has made.
Let all the earth rejoice
Alleluia

Gospel   *Matthew 13:31-32*

Jesus told them this parable: "The kingdom of heaven is like this. A man takes a mustard seed and sows it in his field. It is the smallest of all seeds, but when it grows up, it is the biggest of all plants. It becomes a tree so that birds came and make their nest in its branches."

This is the Gospel of the Lord.

R/. Praise to you, Lord Jesus Christ.

Prayer of the Faithful

[Celebrant] We turn to our generous God whose love has sustained us throughout this year and pray:

R/. Compassionate Lord,
lead us and guide us.

That the Church may continue to bear witness to Christ by deeds of love and compassion.

R/. Compassionate Lord,
lead us and guide us.

That we will all be true witnesses of your love.

R/. Compassionate Lord,
lead us and guide us.

That all who are moving on to new schools will be happy.

R/. Compassionate Lord,
lead us and guide us.

That all our teachers and school staff may be blessed.

R/. Compassionate Lord,
lead us and guide us.

That all who are waiting for results of examinations will receive good news.

R/. Compassionate Lord,
lead us and guide us.

That we will have a happy and safe holiday and use our talents wisely.

R/. Compassionate Lord,
lead us and guide us.

[Celebrant] God of all ages listen to our prayers which we make through Christ our Lord.

R/. Amen.

■ LITURGY OF THE EUCHARIST

Preparation of the Altar and
procession with the gifts   *Music*

Prayer over the Gifts

Lord, we offer you these gifts with gratitude for all the blessings of the past year. May this Eucharist help us to grow closer to you. We ask this through Christ our Lord.

R/. Amen.

Eucharistic Prayer
Masses for Children I.

The Preface tells us that today we give thanks and praise for all God's gifts.

Prayer after Communion

Lord, strengthen us with your Word and Sacrament. Help us as we leave school to serve you in all we meet.
We ask this in the name of Jesus the Lord.

R/. Amen.

OCCASIONS

■ CONCLUDING RITES

Blessing

Dismissal

Recessional hymn

Will you come and follow me
if I can but call your name?
Will you go where you don't know
and never be the same?
Will you let my love be shown,
will you let my name be known,
will you let my life be grown
in you and you in me?

Will you leave yourself behind
if I but call your name?
Will you care for cruel and kind
and never be the same?
Will you risk the hostile stare
should your life attract or scare?
Will you let me answer prayer
in you and you in me?

Lord, your summons echoes true
when you but call my name.
Let me turn and follow you
and never be the same.
In your company I'll go
where your love and footsteps show.
Thus I'll move and live and grow
in you and you in me.

*[Celebration Hymnal for Everyone
no.821 vs.1, 2 and 5]*

© 1986 GIA Publications Inc.

2 TEACHER'S NOTES

Background

THE SCHOOL YEAR is at an end. Last September it looked like a long time until Summer, but the time has passed. We look back on the past year and tie it up. We can of course give thanks for all the good things of the year. We need to thank people too: parents, teachers, priests, staff in the school, our school friends. But it may be a time when we need to let go. We can have suffered hurts, disappointments, difficulties, health problems of our own or people close to us. We may have to forgive people, forgive ourselves for failure and mistakes. Letting go means not carrying negative baggage into the following year.

Central focus

The Eucharist is the source and summit of the Christian life. There is nothing that we cannot bring to the Eucharist: success, failure, sin, weakness, disappointments, hopes, fears, gifts, blessings, sorrows. Jesus is present at Mass to receive us as we are to take us up fully in his love and strength.

Readings

The first reading from Isaiah takes up the theme of God's blessings. The Gospel of the mustard seed alerts us to the fact that we do not know the future, but we are assured that even our smallest efforts can be blessed by God and become significant in his plan.

Offertory

Procession with symbols and gifts:
- ○ Certificates, trophies, awards.
- ○ Mission statement of school.
- ○ School crest/tie/jumper.
- ○ A plant or slip of some tree that can be planted later.
- ○ Photographs of school events.
- ○ Bread and wine.

Eucharistic Prayer
Masses for Children I

The Preface tells us that today we give thanks and praise for all God's gifts.

Sanctus Acclamation *Sung*

Memorial Acclamation *Sung*

Great Amen *Sung*

Communion *Music*

Follow up

Adults say that school days are the happiest days of our lives. Maybe so; maybe not. It is important to be able to look back at school to see what we have learned, not only from books, but from others, from life experience, from mistakes in the past year. We may not always have remembered Jesus in our joys and sorrows; we could be more attentive to his love and presence as we begin holidays and say goodbye to this school year.

---

3 CELEBRANT'S NOTES

Background

INTRODUCTION TO THE MASS

THE CHURCH wants us to mark every week through our celebration of Sunday Mass. There are also important events in life that should be brought to God in praise and thanksgiving, in sorrow or repentance.
The school year will be differently seen by all the pupils. The Mass can be an exercise is seeing how worship and life are to be integrated, how everything is to be brought to God's love.

Readings

The Israelites loved to remember the good things that God had done for his people. Their prayer usually began with thanksgiving for past benefits before going on to pray for present needs. The first reading from Isaiah celebrates God's goodness. The Gospel gives the parable of the mustard seed: a tiny seed grows into a shrub. We do not know how our actions will affect our own lives, or those of other people.

Homily pointers

With awareness of the different experiences that pupils and teachers may have had in the past year, the homily might seek to context the joys and sorrows, the achievements and failures of the year.

○ God's view of things may not be ours.
○ The achievements of a school year are not solely academic: personal values, friendship, caring, dealing with difficulties are all ways in which we mature.
○ Little things are important and can have far-reaching effects.
○ What is important in God's eyes about the past year?
○ Life moves on: we need to give thanks, to forgive, to learn from mistakes.
○ We all experience what Jesus called the Cross; we need to learn how to deal and cope with the hard things of life.
○ Trust in God for the future.

Communion reflection

Tell Jesus about your experience of the past year.

Dismissal

A thankful heart will allow us to develop a positive outlook.

[Thanks to those who prepared the liturgy and participated in it.]

Addresses of copyright holders